Equipping the Church *with* Grief Ministry Skills

A GRIEF MINISTRY SKILLS WORKBOOK

DR. MICHAEL D. BAKER

WESTBOW
P R E S S®
A DIVISION OF THOMAS NELSON
& ZONDERVAN

WestBow Press books may be ordered through booksellers or by contacting:

WestBow Press
A Division of Thomas Nelson & Zondervan
1663 Liberty Drive
Bloomington, IN 47403
www.westbowpress.com
844-714-3454

ISBN: 978-1-6642-4690-4 (sc)
ISBN: 978-1-6642-4691-1 (e)

Library of Congress Control Number: 2021920711

Print information available on the last page.

WestBow Press rev. date: 1/20/2022

Contents

This book is lovingly dedicated to my father,
Bro. Bill Baker,
whose life and ministry influenced many people.

Some people called him the "Pope of Tippah County,"
while others called him the "Funeral Man."
I called him, "Dad."

He lived and served with the motto,
"Love the people, preach the Word, and leave the rest to God."

He entered into his eternal rest on August 16, 2021.

Preface

I want to welcome you and thank you for your interest in this *Grief Ministry Skills Workbook*. This workbook is a five-session course to be used to equip pastors and laity in grief ministry skills. This workbook is a product of my doctoral work, endorsed by New Orleans Baptist Theological Seminary as partial fulfillment of requirements of the doctorate of ministry degree.

Grief ministry has been a big part of my work in the ministry. As a pastor for more than twenty years, I have experienced the loss of family members and friends, many of whom were members of churches that I have pastored. In my role as pastor, a significant part of my ministry has been ministering to those who have grieved the death of a loved one, including performing funeral services for the families.

In addition to grief ministry, I have served as a hospice chaplain for more than five years, ministering to patients and their families in times of sickness and death. Also, as part of my responsibilities in working as a hospice chaplain, I have served as a bereavement coordinator, ministering to families beyond the death event.

Over the last few years, the Lord has been working in my life to make me more sensitive to the needs of those who have suffered the loss of loved ones. Scripture has been important in shaping my sensitivity. Here are some specific verses that have spoken to me:

1. "Jesus wept" (John 11:35 NKJV). Jesus had compassion for those who lost loved ones.
2. "Weep with those who weep" (Rom. 12:15 NKJV). We are called to be compassionate to those who are mournful.
3. "Blessed are those who mourn, for they shall be comforted" (Matt. 5:4 NKJV). The Lord is a comforter of those who mourn.
4. "Blessed be the God and Father of our Lord Jesus Christ, the Father of mercies and God of all comfort, who comforts us in all our tribulation, that we may be able to

comfort those who are in any trouble, with the comfort with which we ourselves are comforted by God" (2 Cor. 1:3-4 NKJV).

This project has been a labor of love for me. It has required more work than I could have imagined, and at the same time the Lord has gifted me for this ministry. With great joy, as well as with great travail, I present *A Grief Ministry Skills Workbook*.

May the Lord bless you throughout the course of this study, and may He equip you for ministry to those who are bereaved.

Introduction

Guidelines for the Workbook Presented as a Workshop

1. Individuals are not required to share.
2. Please be sensitive to others.
3. Practice the art of listening.
4. Please eliminate cross talk.
5. Maintain confidentiality.
6. Understand that it is OK to cry.

Warning: This workshop may bring up memories that you are not prepared to face at this time. It may bring up emotions that you have buried. It may bring up things from your past that are hidden in your subconscious. This is called *grief ambush*, when a grief attack comes on you unexpectedly, as if you are under attack. Theresa Rando says of these grief attacks, "This is an acute upsurge in grief that occurs suddenly and often when least expected, interrupting ongoing activities and temporarily leaving the person out of control."[1]

A Few Basic Definitions Associated with Grief

Let's first distinguish between bereavement, grief, and mourning.

1. *Bereavement*
   a. Melissa M. Kelly: Bereavement literally means "the state of being deprived of someone by death."[2]

---

[1] Theresa Rando, *Grief, Dying, and Death* (Champaign, IL: Research Press Company, 1984), 34.
[2] Melissa M. Kelly, *Grief: Contemporary Theory and the Practice of Ministry* (Minneapolis, MN.: Fortress Press, 2010), 8.

      b.   Alan Wolfelt: Bereavement is "a state caused by loss such as death."[3]

2. *Grief*

      a.   Theresa Rando: Grief is "the process of psychological, social, and somatic reactions to the perception of loss."[4]

      b.   Dr. J. William Worden: Grief is "a person's reaction to bereavement comprised of thoughts, feelings, and behaviors experienced after the loss that change over time."[5]

      c.   John W. James and Russell Friedman: Grief is "the normal and natural reaction to loss of any kind."[6]

3. *Mourning*

      a.   Theresa Rando: Mourning is "the cultural response to loss."[7]

      b.   Dr. J. William Worden: Mourning is "the process that occurs after a loss by which a bereaved person comes to terms with the loss."[8]

      c.   Alan Wolfelt: Mourning is the "outward expression of grief and bereavement."[9]

- For the purpose of this workshop, grief will strictly be referred to in relation to the loss of a loved one through the death experience.
- Authors Donna Reilly Williams and JoAnn Sturzl state, "Grief is part of the human condition, a part of love. The more one loves, the more acute the pain will be at the separation of the loved one."[10]
- We have all been affected by the loss of a loved one. No one is immune, though we wish we were.

The Need for Grief Ministry within Present Culture

A. *"Grief-Avoidant Society"*

    ✦ We live in a culture that avoids grief, as we "live in a culture that cannot face its own despair."[11]

---

[3] Alan Wolfelt, *Death and Grief: A Guide for Clergy* (Muncie, IN.: Accelerated Development Inc., 1984), 1.

[4] Rando, *Grief, Dying, and Death*, 15.

[5] J. William Worden, *Grief Counseling and Grief Therapy,* 5th ed. (New York: Springer Publishing Company, 2018), 39.

[6] John W. James and Russell Friedman, *The Grief Recovery Handbook* (New York: Harper Collins Publishers, 2009), 3.

[7] Rando, *Grief, Dying, and Death*, 15.

[8] Worden, *Grief Counseling*, 5th ed., 39.

[9] Wolfelt, *Death and Grief,* 1.

[10] Donna Reilly Williams and JoAnn Sturzl, *Grief Ministry* (San Jose, CA: Resource Publication, 1992), 35.

[11] Halbert Weidner, *Grief, Loss, and Death: The Shadow Side of Ministry* (Binghamton, NY: The Haworth Press, Inc., 2006), 18.

+ Grieving, "even for those experiencing the greatest loss, is acceptable only for a short period of time."[12]

+ Seemingly, we cannot speak of the loss of a loved one for fear of upsetting someone. Thus, we keep conversation at a shallow level and almost refuse to address the deepest of human emotions.

+ People often ask, "How is the family taking it?" But people do not really want the truth. How would you like it if I responded to that question with, "Well, to tell the truth, they are in the fetal position as if they were kicked in the stomach by a horse" or "They are wrapped in grief, moving in and out of numbness, overwhelmed by uncontrollable tears."[13]

+ The truth is that a lasting state of mourning and grief is unacceptable in our culture; even grieving the loss of a spouse or child is only acceptable for a short time.

+ We live in a grief-avoidant society where it is no longer acceptable to grieve for long periods of time, especially in public.

B. *Culture of Death*
   + Though we have a culture that is grief avoidant, we are bombarded with death.
   + Death is all around us.
     o Real death (deaths that actually take place)
       ▪ It is broadcast in our homes nightly in local, national, and international news through the use of media, whether it be television or internet.
       ▪ It is in the newspapers daily, whether on the front page with local violence or on the back page in the obituaries.
       ▪ It is in our very lives as we lose family, friends, and neighbors on a regular basis.
     o Fictional death (death that is not actual death but imagined through various forms of media)
       ▪ It is in almost every television show or movie, as it is often part of the plot for dramas and action movies.
       ▪ It is frequently seen in video games that adults, children, and youth play.
   + We live in a culture of death that we cannot escape, yet we live in a grief-avoidant society in which we try to escape death.

---

[12] Weidner, *Grief, Loss, and Death,* 19.
[13] Weidner, *Grief, Loss, and Death,* 11, 19.

   C. *Opportunity for Ministry*
- ✦ While living in a culture of death that is grief avoidant, there is great opportunity for ministry.
- ✦ People are hurting and are in need of the comforting presence of the Lord, and often the presence of the Lord is felt through the presence of His church.
- ✦ "Death provides a natural opportunity."[14]
- ✦ "The purpose for which He comforts us is so that we may comfort others.... God comforts us in the midst of our affliction so that we will be better equipped to comfort others."[15] Thus, "suffering expands our ministry" and "suffering authenticates our ministry."[16]
- ✦ The *primary message* of the Bible is that the death, burial, and resurrection of Christ brings hope to sinners.[17]
- ✦ Central to the Bible's message of hope is that "the death of one (Jesus) can bring life to many."[18]
- ✦ As the church, we carry hope to a world that cannot avoid death, no matter how hard it tries.

The Need for the Church to be Equipped to Minister in Present Culture

   A. *Emotional Wellness*
- ✦ Because the church is a part of the very culture of death, often the church mirrors the culture. Thus, church members may also be grief avoidant to the point that grief ministry is not something to which they would naturally be drawn.
- ✦ It is essential that church members working in grief ministry are aware of their own personal grief experiences and have had sufficient healing take place so that they can help others. Thus, the emotional wellness of each member is essential when working with grief sufferers.

---

[14] Paul Tautges, *Comfort Those Who Grieve: Ministering God's Grace in Times of Loss* (Carlisle, PA: Day One Publications, 2009), 12.

[15] Tautges, *Comfort Those Who Grieve*, 51.

[16] Tautges, *Comfort Those Who Grieve*, 64.

[17] Tautges, *Comfort Those Who Grieve*, 96.

[18] Tautges, *Comfort Those Who Grieve*, 69.

B. *Education*
   + Secondly, a need exists for members working in grief ministry to be educated in grief ministry.
   + For a person to work in grief ministry, he or she needs knowledge of basic concepts and terminology in the field of grief.
   + Part of this knowledge base is understanding normal and abnormal symptoms of grief and how to respond accordingly.

C. *Equipping*
   + Third, once the church member is emotionally well from his or her own grief experiences and educated in grief ministry, then he or she must be equipped with sufficient training.
   + The purpose of this workbook is to enhance the ministry skills of pastor and laity so that the church can fulfill Matthew 5:4: "Blessed are those who mourn, for they shall be comforted."
   + Several verses of scripture are instrumental in calling the laity to grief ministry:
     o "...who comforts us in all our tribulation, that we may be able to comfort those who are in any trouble with the comfort with which we ourselves are comforted" (2 Cor. 1:4 NKJV).
     o "Rejoice with those who rejoice, and weep with those who weep" (Rom. 12:15 (NKJV).
     o "Wherefore comfort one another with these words" (1 Thess. 4:18 KJV).
     o "Finally, all of you, be like-minded, be sympathetic, love one another, be compassionate and humble" (1 Pet. 3:8 NIV).
   + The author's desire for the workbook is to enhance the ministry skills of the participants and improve the ministry of the church.

For Reflection and Discussion

- Share your first experience with grief.
- Share your most significant experience of grief.
- Discuss the role of the church in the grieving process.
  o Who ministered to you the most? What did they do that stood out?
  o What specific way did the church minister to you?
  o In what ways were you affected the most by others?
  o What opportunities for the church exist within the present culture?

Prayer for Grief Bearers by Father Mychal Judge

"Lord, take me where You want me to go; Let me meet who You want me to meet; Tell me what You want me to say; and keep me out of your way."[19]

---
[19] Mary M. Toole, *Handbook for Chaplains* (Mahwah, NJ: Paulist Press, 2006), vi.

Session One

Theoretical Foundations of Grief

What Is Grief?

- According to Alan Wolfelt, grief is "an emotional suffering caused by death or another form of bereavement."[20]
- Also, John W. James and Russell Friedman define grief as "the normal and natural reaction to loss of any kind."[21]
- Grief is emotional suffering caused by loss. This study is focused on the loss of a loved one.

Facts about Grief

- Grief is natural.
  - Grief is "the normal and natural reaction to loss of any kind."[22] The most common form of grief is the loss of a loved one through the death event. But it does not have to be related to death. Other common forms of grief can be associated with the loss of a pet, the loss of a marriage through divorce, the loss of a job, the loss of health, etc.
  - Grief is "as natural to every person as breathing. It is inevitable!"[23]

---

[20] Wolfelt, *Death and Grief*, 1.

[21] John W. James and Russell Friedman, *The Grief Recovery Method Handbook* (New York: Harper Collins Publishers, 2009), 3.

[22] James and Friedman, *Grief Recovery Method Handbook*, 3.

[23] Granger E. Westberg, *Good Grief* (Minneapolis: Fortress Press, 2011), 13.

- Grief is unique.
  - Grief is uniquely normal. It is unique to every individual. Yet grief is normal because grief has characteristics that are common to all of us.
  - Cynthia Bailey-Rug states, "Grief is as unique as your fingerprint, and like fingerprints, no two people's grief is exactly alike."[24]
  - We all experience loss, and no one is immune to grieving. In fact, "We all experience loss many times in our lives."[25]
- Grief is universal.
  - Williams and Sturzl state, "Grief is part of the human condition, a part of love. The more one loves, the more acute the pain will be at the separation of the loved one."[26]
  - Kenneth Doka states, "Whatever you love—whether a person, a pet, or even an object—you may one day lose, for loss is a universal occurrence. And when you lose what you love, whether by separation or death, you grieve that loss; so grief, too, is a universal experience."[27]
- Grief is work.
  - Another reality we need to understand is that grief is a process that requires every person to do his or her own grief work.
  - The term "grief work" was coined by Eric Lindemann in the 1940s. In his research, he determined that grief was work because it "requires the expenditure of both physical and emotional energy."[28]
  - Grief work is the "activity [or activities] associated with thinking through the loss, facing its reality, expressing the feelings and emotions experienced, and becoming re-involved in life."[29]
  - Grief is a process that requires every person to do his or her own grief work. No one can do it for you.

Theories of Grief

A. *Attachment Theory*

---

[24] Cynthia Bailey-Rug, *Emerging from the Chrysalis* (Morrisville, NC: Lulu Publishing, 2012), 113.
[25] James and Friedman, *The Grief Recovery Method Handbook*, 7.
[26] Williams and Sturzl, *Grief Ministry*, 35.
[27] Kenneth J. Doka, *Grief Is a Journey* (New York: Atria Books, 2016), 1.
[28] Rando, *Grief, Dying, and Death*, 20.
[29] J. William Worden, *Grief Counseling and Grief Therapy*, 4th ed. (New York, NY: Springer Publishing Company, 2009), 13.

- Attachment theory is a "theory that suggests that there are fundamental reasons for the ways humans react to grief."[30]
- In John Bowlby's study of grief, he looked at the development of attachments within family relationships, particularly in the relationship between children and their parents. He noted that humans have a tendency to "create strong affectional bonds with others," and he attempted to "understand the strong emotional reaction that occurs when those bonds are threatened or broken."[31]
- Bowlby noted that when an attachment figure disappears, "the response is one of intense anxiety and strong emotional protest."[32] Thus, "the greater the potential for loss, the more intense and the more varied the reaction."[33] In simple terms, the greater the love, the greater the loss. The greater the attachment, the greater the grief.
- Essentially, "when an individual cares about someone, he emotionally invests part of himself in that person. In psychoanalytic terms this is called cathexis. There is an emotional bond between the person and whoever he cares about that develops as that individual invests his psychic and emotional energy in the loved one. When one of the people dies, the remaining person has to withdraw the emotional energy that was invested in the person who is no longer alive."[34] It is easily understood that the greater the attachment, the more difficulty one will have in the detaching (*decathexis*).
- The various stages of grief, or phases of grief, or tasks of grief, are all theories that attempt to describe the processing of grief that comes with detaching from the deceased, experiencing the pain of the loss, and eventually adjusting to life without the attachment and establishing a new normal.

B. *Tasks of Mourning*

- Dr. J. William Worden has been one of the most prominent researchers in the field of grief over the last half century. His work in the field of developmental psychology has influenced many modern grief theorists.
- While many grief theorists have promoted their findings as stages or phases, Worden chooses to recognize the process of grief as tasks to accomplish rather than stages to experience.

---

[30] Rando, *Grief, Dying, and Death*, 21.
[31] Worden, *Grief Counseling*, 5th ed., 15.
[32] Worden, *Grief Counseling*, 5th ed., 16.
[33] Worden, *Grief Counseling*, 5th ed., 16.
[34] Rando, *Grief, Dying, and Death*, 18.

- Worden views the theories of stages and phases as experienced passively, as if it is "something that the mourner must pass through."[35]
- In contrast, Worden's theory on tasks of mourning focuses on the mourner's ability to take action and do something, which "gives the mourner some sense of leverage and hope that there is something that he or she can actively do to adapt to the death of a loved one."[36]
- Worden sees mourning as the adaptation to loss involving four basic tasks: (1) accept the reality of the loss, (2) process the pain of the loss, (3) adjust to the world without the deceased, and (4) find a way to remember the deceased while embarking on the rest of one's journey through life.[37]

C. *Continuing Bonds*
- In 1996, Dennis Klass, Phyllis Silverman, and Steven Nickman wrote *Continuing Bonds: New Understandings in Grief (Death Education, Aging, and Health Care)*. They coined the phrase "continuing bonds."[38]
- In their work, they broke from the traditional examination of grief as distinct phases or stages and looked at the continuing relationship that often exists with the deceased.
- It was their understanding that "a sense of continuing bond with a deceased person is not pathological but rather seems to be a source of great comfort and healing."[39]
- They acknowledged that the continuing bonds can take many forms:
  1. First, the person may "live on in the memory."[40]
  2. Second, the continuing bond is "our sense of the legacy that a deceased person has left; that is, the many ways they have touched us and continue to touch and influence us."[41]
  3. Third, "some people feel that their deceased loved ones watch over and protect them."[42]
- In ministering to the bereaved, one must be careful and sensitive in the understanding of continuing bonds.

---

[35] Worden, *Grief Counseling*, 5th ed., 40.
[36] Worden, *Grief Counseling*, 5th ed., 40
[37] Worden, *Grief Counseling*, 5th ed., 41–50.
[38] Melissa Kelly, Grief: *Contemporary Theory and Practice of Ministry* (Minneapolis, Minn.:Fortress Press, 2010), 25.
[39] Melissa Kelly, page 25.
[40] Melissa Kelly, page 25.
[41] Melissa Kelly, page 25.
[42] Melissa Kelly, page 25.

- As Melissa Kelly states, "While one may draw comfort and meaning from a sense of ongoing connection to the deceased, one must still move into one's future with hope and trust in God's promises," realizing that the "real and ongoing presence of Christ in our lives is the ultimate continuing bond."[43]

D. *Dual Process Model*
- Another prominent theory of grief is the "dual process of grief model" developed by Margarate Stroebe and Henk Schut.[44]
- In their study, they theorized that the grief work hypothesis fell short of being effective in coping with bereavement.
- Instead, Stroebe and Schut found that there are two emotional processes that represent human grief: loss-oriented and restoration-oriented processes.
- In the loss-oriented process, people express grief through powerful grief-related emotions, while in the restoration-oriented process, people are adjusting to new roles and responsibilities without their loved ones.
- According to Stroebe and Schut, people *oscillate* between these two emotional processes.
- The two processes are what give us the name of the *dual process model.*
- The important thing to remember is that the dual process model relies on balance, with too much focus on either process being potentially unhealthy.

E. *Meaning Reconstruction*
- One of the latest models of grief therapy is that of meaning reconstruction, which was developed by Robert Neimeyer. In his work as a contemporary grief theorist, Neimeyer sees the "affirmation and/or reconstruction of meaning after loss as the central process in grieving."[45]
- Neimeyer opposed the cookie-cutter approach to grief offered by stage theorists, citing a lack of scientific evidence for the stage theory. His primary interest was in reconstruction of meaning after loss, believing that we as humans are "meaning makers."[46]

---

[43] Melissa Kelly, page 26.

[44] Margaret Strobe and Henk Schut, "The Dual Process Model of Coping with Bereavement: A Decade On," *OMEGA—Journal of Death and Dying* 61, no. 4 (2010), 273–289.

[45] Melissa Kelly, page 3.

[46] Melissa Kelly, page 76.

- According to author Melissa Kelly, we make meaning through the narrative of our life story. Experiencing loss "can disrupt some or all of the elements of our story, thereby threatening our meaning system."[47]
- According to Neimeyer's meaning reconstruction theory, "grieving individuals can be viewed as struggling to affirm or reconstruct a personal world of meaning that has been challenged by loss."[48]
- In his work with Diana C. Sands, Neimeyer states, "In the aftermath of life-altering loss, the bereaved are commonly precipitated into a search for meaning …"[49]
- Ultimately, the loss of a loved one will result in the reconstruction of meaning, which will revise the narrative of the grief sufferer.
- According to Neimeyer, the reconstruction of the narrative through "meaning making" contributes to the resolution of grief as the grief sufferer adapts to the loss. As such, the person's life story changes with every loss and reconstruction of meaning.[50]

F. *Grieving Styles*
- Another relatively new theory of grief has been developed by Dr. Kenneth Doka.
- In his work, *Grieving Beyond Gender*, Dr. Doka established two types of grieving styles: "on one end are people who tend to be *instrumental* in their grief, whereas on the other end are individuals who may be considered *intuitive*."[51]
- According to Doka, "Intuitive grievers experience grief primarily as waves of affect expressing this grief in a variety of ways, such as crying or ventilating affect. Finding appropriate ways to ventilate this affect is a useful adaptive strategy that facilitates their grieving process."[52] In this style of grieving, "feelings are intensely experienced and expressed."[53]
- Additionally, instrumental grievers experience grief in other ways. Affect is usually modulated, and they tend to describe grief more in physical, behavioral, or cognitive manifestations. Expressions of grief tend to be active and cognitive. Useful adaptive strategies for instrumental grievers will be drawn from more cognitive and active

---

[47] Melissa Kelly, page 81.
[48] Melissa Kelly, page 83.
[49] Robert A. Neimeyer and Diana C. Sands, "Meaning Reconstruction in Bereavement," in *Grief and Bereavement in Contemporary Society*, ed. Robert A. Neimeyer, Darcy L. Harris, Howard R. Winokuer, and Gordon F. Thornton (New York: Routledge Taylor & Francis Group, 2011), 11.
[50] Niemeyer and Sands, "Meaning Reconstruction in Bereavement," 11.
[51] Kenneth Doka, *Grieving Beyond Gender* (New York: Routledge Taylor and Francis Group, 2010), 201.
[52] Doka, *Grieving Beyond Gender*, 201.
[53] Doka, *Grieving Beyond Gender*, xvi.

approaches."[54] With instrumental grievers, "thinking is predominant to feelings, there is a general reluctance to talk about emotions, and mastery of oneself and the environment is sought, often accomplished through problem solving and directed activity."[55]

- In his book, *Grief Is a Journey*, Dr. Doka acknowledges four major patterns of grieving:[56]
  - o Heart grievers—You may be more intuitive in your grief. You tend to experience, express, and cope with grief more *emotionally*.
  - o Head grievers—You may be more instrumental in your grief, experiencing, expressing, and adapting to it in more *cognitive* or active ways.
  - o Heart and head grievers—You have both types of reaction to grief and move back and forth between the two.
  - o Heart versus head grievers—You feel constrained about expressing grief. This is called dissonant pattern. There is dissonance or disconnection between how you experience and how you express your grief.
- According to Doka, "Differences in patterns are differences, not deficiencies. Each pattern, depending on the way it is utilized as well as the societal expectations about grief- can complicate or facilitate the grieving process."[57]

The Process of Grief

- Many researchers have worked to define the grief process over the last century: Sigmund Freud in 1917, Erich Lindemann in 1944, Elizabeth Kubler-Ross in 1969, John Bowlby in 1980, J. William Worden in 1982, and Theresa Rando in 1984. We will look briefly at a few of them.
- First, Elizabeth Kubler Ross and her now-famous *five stages of grief:*
  - o Denial and isolation (shock)—a period of shock that functions as a buffer against overwhelming reality of the situation.
  - o Anger
  - o Bargaining—a stage in which pleas are made to God or the doctor to forestall the loss, or behaviors are undertaken to avoid grieving over it after it has occurred.
  - o Depression

---

[54] Doka, *Grieving Beyond Gender*, 201
[55] Doka, *Grieving Beyond Gender*, xvi.
[56] Doka, *Grief Is a Journey*, 85-90.
[57] Doka, *Grieving Beyond Gender*, 202.

- o Acceptance[58]
  - ▪ Not all researchers agree with Ross's finding, citing that not all people exhibit all the stages of grief. What many people do not know is that Ross worked primarily with dying patients who were experiencing anticipatory grief.
  - ▪ Though not everyone agrees with Ross's findings concerning grief, most would agree that Ross's work was instrumental in bringing heightened awareness about the process of dying.
- Second, John Bowlby and Colin Murray Parkes believed that the grief process included *four phases of grief*:
  - o Phase of numbness—a stage of being stunned.
  - o Phase of yearning and searching—a phase that includes anger, fruitless searching, disbelief, restlessness, and irritability.
  - o Phase of disorganization and despair—a phase characterized by the person giving up the search, accompanied by depression and despair.
  - o Phase of reorganization—a phase that sees the bereaved reestablish new ties to others, with a gradual return of interests and appetites. [59]
- Third is Theresa Rando's *phases of reaction* to loss:[60]
  - o Avoidance phase—This phase includes a strong desire to avoid the acknowledgement of the loss, in which there is shock, denial, and disbelief.
  - o Confrontation phase—This phase includes the confrontation of the reality of loss and often includes anger and guilt. This is when grief is most intense and highly emotional.
  - o Reestablishment phase—This phase includes the gradual decline of the grief and the beginning of an emotional and social reentry back into the everyday world.
- Fourth comes J. William Worden's *four tasks of grief*:
  - o Task 1: Accept the reality of the loss. Worden states that "[t]he first task of grieving is to come full face with the reality that the person is dead, that the person is gone."[61]
  - o Task 2: Experience the pain of grief. Worden states that "[n]ot everyone experiences the same intensity of pain or feels it in the same way, but it is nearly impossible to lose someone to whom you have been deeply attached without experiencing some level of pain."[62]

---

[58] Rando, *Grief, Dying, and Death*, 27.
[59] Rando, *Grief, Dying, and Death*, 25.
[60] Rando, *Grief, Dying, and Death*, 29-36.
[61] Worden, *Grief Counseling*, th ed., 41.
[62] Worden, *Grief Counseling*, 5th ed., 45.

- o Task 3: Adjust to a world without the deceased that includes three adjustments:
  - External adjustments—adjusting to a new environment without the deceased.[63]
  - Internal adjustments—adjusting to one's own sense of self as death affects self-definition, self-esteem, and self-efficacy.[64]
  - Spiritual adjustments—adjusting to the loss of a loved one can lead a person to a spiritual crisis, where beliefs are challenged at the foundations of one's assumptive world.[65]
- o Task 4: Find a way to remember the deceased while embarking on the rest of one's journey through life. Worden states, "We need to find ways to memorialize, that is to remember dead loved ones—keeping them with us but still going on with life." [66]

Three Bereavement Trajectories for Recovery

- Some modern grief theorists dispute the idea of psychological stages, with certain researchers believing that stage theory has been "put to rest."[67]
- These researchers believe that "bereavement trajectories form curvilinear paths, and among adults involve basic groupings: a majority of persons who are resilient, a large plurality that struggles but recovers, and a small minority whose grief goes unabated without intervention."[68]
- According to Dr. George Bonanno, bereavement follows three trajectories.[69]
  - o The first trajectory are *resilient people* who "quickly return to living productive lives and to loving the persons around them." This accounts for 45-50 percent of all grief sufferers.
  - o The second trajectory are individuals who are *struggling but recover*. These individuals are "persons moving only gradually from intense distress to eventual recovery; it takes at least 2 years to regain one's equilibrium." Bonanno further states that this trajectory accounts for about 40 percent of bereaved individuals.

---

[63] Worden, *Grief Counseling*, 5th ed., 47.
[64] Worden, *Grief Counseling*, 5th ed., 48.
[65] Worden, *Grief Counseling*, 5th ed., 49.
[66] Worden, *Grief Counseling*, 5th ed., 50.
[67] David E. Balk, "Life Span Issues and Loss, Grief, and Mourning: Adulthood" in *Handbook of Thanatology*, 2nd ed., ed. David K. Meagher and David E. Balk (New York: Routledge, 2013), 158-159.
[68] Balk, *Life Span Issues*, 158.
[69] Balk, *Life Span Issues*, 158-159.

o The third trajectory is that of *complicated grief.* For these individuals, "bereavement overwhelms them, and unless they receive effective intervention, they remain in acute grief for years. People in this trajectory withdraw from the world and become mired in an endless preoccupation, an insatiable desire to have the deceased back again." People in this trajectory account for 10-15 percent of bereaved individuals.

Various Types of Grief

- Abbreviated grief—This is a "short lived, normal form of grief."[70] It may occur because of the immediate replacement of the lost person, such as remarrying shortly after the loss. It may occur as a result of having an extended time to prepare for the death event with anticipatory grief. In abbreviated grief, it appears that the process seems to be worked through quicker than "normal."
- Absent grief—This is when grief does not occur as expected, and the mourner may not demonstrate the ability to grieve. According to Theresa Rando, "In this situation feelings of grief and mourning processes are totally absent. It is as if the death never occurred at all. It requires that the mourner completely deny the death or that he may remain in the stage of shock."[71]
- Acute grief—According to Wolfelt, acute grief is "the intense grief which immediately follows the loss."[72] This is the sudden overwhelming grief that comes upon a person at the loss of a loved one.
- Anticipatory grief—This is the grief that begins before the death of a loved one, as death is imminent. Per Rando, "In the anticipation of a future loss a form of normal grief can occur."[73] Thus, with the awareness of the future loss, a person begins the grieving process before the loss occurs.
- Chronic grief—This is when the grief sufferer continues to exhibit grief responses that were appropriate in the early stages of grief. (This is particularly prevalent in the loss of a spouse, because of the intensity of feelings.) According to Rando, "Mourning fails to draw to its natural conclusion and it almost seems that the bereaved keeps the deceased alive with grief."[74]

---

[70] Rando, *Grief, Dying, and Death,* 62.
[71] Rando, *Grief, Dying, and Death,* 59.
[72] Alan D. Wolfelt, *Death and Grief,* 2.
[73] Rando, *Grief, Dying, and Death,* 37.
[74] Rando, *Grief, Dying, and Death,* 61.

- *Compound grief*—When you have more than one loss at a time, grief is compounded (stacked). When a person suffers more than one loss, grief can be complicated and remain unresolved, being too much for one person to cope with.
- *Conflicted grief*—This is where grief develops in such a way that there may be an "exaggeration or distortion of one or more of the manifestations of normal grief, while other aspects are suppressed. Two common patterns are extreme anger and extreme guilt. This grief reaction can be abnormally prolonged and is often associated with a previously dependent or ambivalent relationship with the deceased."[75]
- *Delayed grief*—This is where "normal or conflicted grief may be delayed for an extended period of time, up to years, especially if there are pressing responsibilities or the mourner feels he cannot deal with the process at the time."[76] For the mourner that delays grief, it may resurface years later, possibly triggered by another loss.
- *Disenfranchised grief*—According to Kenneth Doka, "these losses are at least typically not recognized and supported by others. Disenfranchised losses are not openly acknowledged, socially sanctioned, or publicly shared."[77] For example, you might have a loss that you cannot grieve publicly, such as the loss of a homosexual child in a homophobic culture. Another example is grief for the loss of a lover in an adulterous relationship, which cannot be openly expressed by attendance at the funeral.
- *Normal grief*—Normal grief, also referred to as uncomplicated grief, "encompasses a broad range of feelings and behaviors that are common after a loss."[78] These are commonly experienced behaviors that are frequent in most grief experiences.
- *Unanticipated grief*—This occurs after a sudden, unexpected loss and renders the griever unable to grasp the full implications of the loss. According to Rando, "It occurs after a sudden, unanticipated loss and is so disruptive that recovery is complicated. In unanticipated grief, mourners are unable to grasp the full implications of the loss."[79] With unanticipated grief there is difficulty accepting the loss, despite understanding the reality of the death.
- *Unresolved grief*—This is grief that remains uncompleted, or "unresolved." Grief is unresolved because "[t]here is something that is impeding the mourning process and not allowing it to move forward toward a good adaptation to the loss."[80] For whatever

---

[75] Rando, *Grief, Dying, and Death*, 60.
[76] Rando, *Grief, Dying, and Death*, 60.
[77] Doka, *Grief Is a Journey,* 183.
[78] Worden, *Grief Counseling*, 5th ed., 18.
[79] Rando, *Grief, Dying, and Death*, 61.
[80] Worden, *Grief Counseling*, 5th ed., 141-142.

reason, the grief sufferer is unable to work through his or her grief to the point of recovery.

Normal Grief Symptoms (As Presented by Dr. J. William Worden)

A. *Emotional Symptoms (Feelings)*[81]
- Sadness—This is the most common feeling found in the grief sufferer, often manifested by crying.
- Anger—This is another common behavior experienced after the loss of a loved one. Often anger comes from two sources: "From a sense of frustration that there was nothing one could do to prevent the death, and from a kind of regressive experience that occurs after the loss of someone close."
- Guilt—This emotion is a common experience of survivors. Usually the guilt is "manifested over something that happened or something that was neglected around the time of the death, something that may have prevented the loss. Most often the guilt is irrational."
- Anxiety—This common grief experience can "range from a light sense of insecurity to a strong panic attack, and the more intense and persistent the anxiety, the more it suggests an abnormal grief reaction."
- Loneliness—This feeling of being alone is a frequently expressed feeling, especially for those "who have lost a spouse and who were used to a close day-to-day relationship."
- Fatigue—Defined as a feeling of tiredness that may appear as "apathy or listlessness," grief drains the grief sufferer of energy and strength.
- Helplessness—This feeling of helplessness often incapacitates the grief sufferer and is "frequently present in the early stage of a loss."
- Shock—This emotion occurs "most often in the case of a sudden death."
- Yearning—Normally referred to as "pining," this is a normal response to grief and is frequently found in widows.
- Emancipation (relief, freedom)—After a loss, people often find themselves experiencing the positive feelings associated with a freedom from constraints. Many people "feel relief after the death of a loved one, particularly if the loved one suffered a lengthy or particularly painful illness."
- Numbness—It is common that "some people report a lack of feelings. After a loss, they feel numb." Studies show that this numbness is a defense mechanism to prevent the overwhelming pain of the total weight of the loss.

---

[81] Worden, *Grief Counseling*, 5th ed., 20-24.

B. *Physical Symptoms (Sensations)*[82]
- Hollowness in the stomach
- Tightness in the chest
- Tightness in the throat
- Oversensitivity to noise
- Breathlessness
- Muscle weakness
- Lack of energy
- Dry mouth

C. *Cognitive Symptoms (Cognitions)*[83]
- Disbelief—Grief sufferers often react to their loss with disbelief, as if the loss never occurred.
- Confusion—Grief sufferers often become very confused; "they can't seem to order their thoughts, they have difficulty concentrating or they forget things."
- Preoccupation—This exhibits in the form of "obsessive thoughts about the deceased."
- Sense of presence—This occurs when the "grieving person may think that the deceased is somehow still in the current area of time and space."
- Hallucinations—These include both audible and visible types.

D. *Behavioral Symptoms (Behaviors)*[84]
- Sleep disturbances—These may include the inability to sleep or sleeping too much.
- Eating disturbances—These may include overeating or undereating, but most commonly exists in the form of undereating.
- Absentminded behavior—The grief sufferer may have difficulty paying attention, as if he or she is absentminded.
- Social withdrawal—"It is not unusual for people who have sustained a loss to want to withdraw from other people."
- Dreams of the deceased—"It is very common to dream of the dead person, both normal kinds of dreams and distressing dreams or nightmares."
- Avoiding reminders of the deceased—"Some people will avoid places or things that trigger painful feelings of grief."

---

[82] Worden, *Grief Counseling*, 5th ed., 25.
[83] Worden, *Grief Counseling*, 5th ed., 24-26.
[84] Worden, *Grief Counseling*, 5th ed., 27–31.

- Searching and calling out—This involves the sporadic tendency to call out a person's name, such as "John, John, John. Please come back to me."
- Sighing—Surprisingly, this is a frequent behavior of a grief sufferer, deep sighs as if one is breathless.
- Restless hyperactivity—Nervous energy can lead to over-activity and restlessness.
- Crying—Some grief theorists believe that tears have "potential healing value."
- Visiting places or carrying objects that remind the survivor of the deceased—Instead of avoiding places that remind a grief sufferer of his or her loved one, in some cases, the grief sufferer will visit places or hold onto objects that serve as reminders. The underlying nature of this behavior is the "fear of losing memories of the deceased."
- Treasuring objects that belonged to the deceased—A grief sufferer often treasures objects that belonged to the deceased, as if worshiping the object and keeping the grief sufferer's memory alive.

What Do You Need to Know About Grieving?

A. Authors John W. James and Russell Friedman give practical wisdom for dealing with grief in their book, *The Grief Recovery Method*.[85] These excerpts from their book give the trained counselor or the untrained comforter wisdom for helping the grief sufferer.
- Grief is "the normal and natural reaction to loss of any kind."
- "While grief is normal and natural, and clearly the most powerful of human emotions, it is also the most neglected and misunderstood experience, often by both the grievers and those around them."
- Grief is "the conflicting feelings caused by the end of, or change in, a familiar pattern."
- Yet in modern life, moving through intense emotional pain has become such a misunderstood process that most of us have very little idea of how to respond to loss.
- The death of a loved one produces emotions that can be described as the feeling of reaching out for someone who has always been there, only to find that when we need them one more time, they are no longer there.
- Intensifying the problem, many factors can compound our reactions to loss and limit our recovery.
- Loss is inevitable. We are all likely to face several major losses in our lives. Sometimes loss is even predictable. In spite of these truths, we receive no formal training in how

---

[85] James and Friedman, *Grief Recovery Method Handbook*, 3-8, 11, 24-25, 39-49.

to respond to events that are guaranteed to happen and are sure to cause pain and disruption.

- Often those who want help are ill-prepared to help others deal with loss:
  o They do not know what to say.
  o They are afraid of our feelings.
  o They try to change the subject.
  o They intellectualize.
  o They don't hear us.
  o They don't want to talk about death.
  o They want us to keep our faith.
- James and Friedman identify certain behaviors that they call STERBs: short-term energy relieving behaviors.
- Common STERBs when experiencing grief:
  + food (either eating too much or not enough)
  + alcohol/drugs
  + anger
  + exercise
  + fantasy (movies, TV, books)
  + isolation
  + sex
  + shopping (retail therapy)
  + workaholism
- Three main problems with STERBs.[86]
  o They appear to work. They create an illusion of recovery by causing you to forget or bury emotions.
  o They are short-term. They do not last, and they do not deal with the true emotional issue.
  o They do nothing to remove the cork that is jammed in the spout. In fact, most people do not even realize that there is a cork in the spout.

B. Norman H. Wright, author of *Reflections of a Grieving Spouse,* is an excellent resource for those who have lost their spouses. In his book, he outlines several helpful points of wisdom for after experiencing a loss.[87]

---

[86] James and Friedman, *Grief Recovery Method Handbook*, 80-81.
[87] Norman H. Wright, *Reflections of a Grieving Spouse* (Eugene, OR: Harvest House Publishers, 2009), 76.

- Your grief will take longer than most people think. (Recovering from the loss of a spouse, whether through death or divorce, will likely take three to five years.)[88]
- Your grief will take more energy than you ever imagined.
- Your grief will involve many changes and will continue to develop.
- Your grief will show in all spheres of your life.
- Your grief will depend on how you perceive the loss.
- You will grieve for many things, symbolic and tangible, not just for the death alone.
- You will grieve for what you have lost already and for what you have lost for the future.
- Your grief will entail mourning, not only for the person you lost but also for the hopes, dreams, and unfulfilled expectations you held for and with that person, as well as for unmet needs because of the death.
- Your grief will involve a wide variety of feelings and reactions, more than just the general ones often depicted, such as depression and sadness.
- Your loss will resurrect old issues, feelings, and unresolved conflicts from the past.
- You may experience a combination of anger and depression, which may exhibit as irritability, frustration, annoyance, and intolerance.
- You will feel some anger and guilt or at least some manifestation of these emotions.
- You may experience grief spasms—acute upsurges of grief that occur without warning.
- You will have trouble thinking about memories, handling organizational tasks, intellectually processing information, and making decisions.
- You may feel like you are going insane. Norman H. Wright says, "If you are experiencing intense grief, the 'insane feelings' are actually a sane response!"[89]
- You may be obsessed with the death and preoccupied with the deceased.
- Others will have unrealistic expectations about your mourning and may respond inappropriately to you.

C. Kenneth Doka: *The Myths and Realities of Grief*[90]
- Myth 1: Grief is a predictable process. (It's *not*!)
  - o Reality: Grief is individual. Every loss we experience is unique.
- Myth 2: There is a timetable to grief. (Nope!)
  - o Reality: There is simply no timetable to grief.
- Myth 3: Grief is about letting go. (Not really!)
  - o Reality: We retain a continuing bond with those we love.

---

[88] Williams and Sturzl, *Grief Ministry*, 40.
[89] Wright, *Reflections of a Grieving Spouse*, 20.
[90] Doka, *Grief Is a Journey*, 9-25.

- Myth 4: After a loss, we need closure
  - Reality: There can never be "closure."
- Myth 5: We need to process the loss in order to reach resolution.
  - Reality: We each process loss in our own way.
- Myth 6: Human beings are naturally resilient to loss.
  - Reality: Many individuals are resilient in experiencing loss, yet many find grief difficult, even disabling.
- Myth 7: It is easier to accept a death after a prolonged illness.
  - Reality: All deaths are difficult.

For Reflection and Discussion

- What caught your attention the most in this section?
- What surprised you the most?
- Where did you see yourself in this chapter?
- Did you find yourself agreeing or disagreeing with certain items?

Theoretical Foundations of Unresolved/Complicated Grief

Terminology for Unresolved/Complicated Grief

- Theresa Rando uses the word *unresolved* because "there has been some disturbance of the normal progress towards resolution."[91]
- Alan D. Wolfelt uses the term *complicated*. His personal bias is to "suggest that the terms pathological, abnormal, unresolved, and atypical not be used at all." The basis for his thinking is that the terms are confusing because grief has so many dimensions and varies from person to person.[92]
- J. William Worden prefers the term *complicated mourning* to the term *abnormal grief*. As Worden puts it, "Complicated mourning manifests in several forms and has been given different labels. It is sometimes called pathological, unresolved grief, complicated grief, chronic grief, delayed grief, or exaggerated grief."[93]
- For the purposes of this study, we will use the terms *unresolved* and *complicated* interchangeably.
- Why spend an entire session on "unresolved/complicated" grief?

---

[91] Rando, *Grief, Dying, and Death*, 59.
[92] Wolfelt, *Death and Grief*, 87.
[93] Worden, *Grief Counseling*, 5th ed.,137.

- First, there is a likelihood that we will meet people who are struggling with unresolved grief and who need help.
- Secondly, and most importantly, we must be healthy enough to help others.

Examining Your Own Grief

- In training grief counselors, J. William Worden gives several reasons for grief counselors to examine their own grief.[94]
  - First, "working with the bereaved may make us aware, sometimes painfully so, of our own losses."
  - Second, a grief counselor may have to face his or her "feared losses." As Worden states, "If the loss our client is experiencing is similar to the one we most fear, our apprehension can get in the way of an effective counseling relationship."
  - Third, working with the grieving may make a grief counselor painfully aware of "one's own personal death."
- Why do we need to examine our own grief? If we are to help others, we must have resolved the grief we have experienced to the point that we can help others and not harm them.

What Is "Unresolved Grief" or "Complicated Grief"?

- According to J. William Worden, it is "the intensification of grief to the level where the person is overwhelmed, resorts to maladaptive behavior, or remains terminally in the state of grief without progression of the mourning process towards completion."[95]
- According to C. Charles Bachmann, "Grief can be expressed, repressed, or suppressed, for these are the ways of dealing with emotions." Bachmann also states, "Full expression will never cause mental illness. It is, again, a curious part of our cultural heritage here in America that we put a premium on the stoic concealment of emotional reaction patterns. Giving vent to feelings through tears or verbal expression is the best mental health insurance." Bachmann further states that "[t]hough no accurate statistics are available, it has been estimated that about 10 percent of the admissions to mental hospitals are persons suffering from unresolved grief problems related to bereavement."[96]

---

[94] Worden, *Grief Counseling*, 4th ed., 252.
[95] Worden, *Grief Counseling*, 4th ed., 134.
[96] C. Charles Bachmann, *Ministering to the Grief Sufferer* (Englewood Cliffs, NJ: Prentice-Hall, Inc., 1964), 13, 18.

What Are the Common *Types* of Unresolved/Complicated Grief?

- According to Theresa Rando, there are seven types of unresolved grief.[97]
  - Absent grief—"In this situation feelings of grief and mourning processes are totally absent."
  - Inhibited grief—"In this form, there is a lasting inhibition (hang-up, shyness) of many of the manifestations of normal grief, with the appearance of other symptoms such as somatic (relating to the body) complaints in their place."
  - Delayed grief—"Normal or conflicted grief may be delayed for an extended period of time, up to years, especially if there are pressing responsibilities or the mourner feels he cannot deal with the process at that time."
  - Conflicted grief—"In this grief there is frequently an exaggeration or distortion of one or more of the manifestations of normal grief, while other aspects of the grief may be suppressed at the same time."
  - Chronic grief—"In chronic grief the mourner continuously exhibits intense grief reactions that would be appropriate in the early stages of loss. Mourning fails to draw to its natural conclusion and it almost seems that the bereaved keeps the deceased alive with grief."
  - Unanticipated grief—Unanticipated grief happens "after a sudden, unanticipated loss and is so disruptive that recovery is usually complicated. In unanticipated grief, mourners are unable to grasp the full implications of the loss."
  - Abbreviated grief—"This reaction is often mistaken for unresolved grief. In fact, it is a short-lived but normal form of grief."
- Alan D. Wolfelt acknowledges four types of unresolved grief.[98]
  - Absent grief—"In absent grief no apparent feelings of grief are expressed. The person may project a picture as if the death never occurred."
  - Distorted grief—"In distorted grief, a distortion occurs in one or more of the normal dimensions of grief. This distortion may prevent the grief process from unfolding and the person often becomes fixated on the distorted dimension of grief." The most common dimensions of grief that become distorted are anger and guilt.
  - Converted grief—"In converted grief the person demonstrates behaviors and symptoms which result in personal distress: however, he or she is unable to relate their presence to the loss." For example, a person may unconsciously convert the emotional pain of his or her grief to the physical pain of a mysterious illness.

---

[97] Rando, *Grief, Dying, and Death*, 59-61, 91.
[98] Wolfelt, Alan D. *Death and Grief: A Guide for Clergy*, 87.

- o Chronic grief—"In chronic grief the person demonstrates a persistent pattern of intense grief that does not result in appropriate reconciliation (resolution)."

What *Grief Reactions* Contribute to Unresolved Grief?

- According to J. William Worden, there are four common grief reactions that contribute to unresolved grief.[99]
  - o Chronic grief reactions—"A chronic or prolonged grief reaction is one that is excessive in duration and never comes to a satisfactory conclusion." For example, anniversary reactions may last as long as ten years.
  - o Delayed grief reactions—These are "sometimes called inhibited, suppressed, or postponed grief reactions. In this case, the person may have had an emotional reaction at the time of the loss, but it is not sufficient to the loss. At a future date, the person may experience symptoms of grief …"
  - o Exaggerated grief reactions—This reaction "has to do with exaggerated grief responses in which the people experiencing the intensification of a normal grief reaction either feels overwhelmed or resorts to maladaptive behavior." An example of this would be clinical depression.
  - o Masked grief reactions—With this reaction, patients "experience symptoms and behaviors that cause them difficulty, but they do not recognize the fact that these symptoms or behaviors are related to the loss."

What Are Common *Symptoms* of Unresolved/Complicated Grief?

- In Erich Lindemann's original study in 1944, he identified nine symptoms of unresolved/complicated grief.[100]
  - o overactivity without a sense of loss
  - o acquisition of symptoms belonging to the last illness of the deceased.
  - o development of a psychosomatic medical illness (physical illness manifested in the mind)
  - o alteration in relationships with friends and relatives
  - o furious hostility against specific persons somehow connected with the death

---

[99] Worden, *Grief Counseling*, 5th ed., 142-147.
[100] Rando, *Grief, Dying, and Death*, 62-65.

- o wooden and formal conduct that masks hostile feelings
- o lasting loss of patterns of social interaction
- o acts detrimental to one's own social and economic existence
- o agitated depression with tension, agitation, insomnia, feelings of worthlessness, bitter self-accusation, and obvious need for punishment
- In 1982, J. William Worden identified additional symptoms:
- o a relatively minor event triggering major grief reactions
- o false euphoria subsequent to the death
- o over-identification with the deceased, leading to a compulsion to imitate the dead person, particularly if it is unconscious and the mourner lacks the competence for the same behavior
- o self-destructive impulses
- o radical changes in lifestyle
- o exclusion of friends, family members, or activities associated with the deceased
- o phobias about illness or death

What Are Some Common *Causes* of Unresolved Grief?

Theresa Rando outlines both psychological and social factors in unresolved grief.

A. *Psychological Factors in Unresolved Grief* [101]
- Guilt—"Unresolved grief may occur when mourners are afraid to grieve because reviewing their relationship with the deceased would bring up negative acts or feelings they had directed toward her, or things they had neglected to do, making them feel guilty."
- Loss of an extension of the self—"Some people may be so dependent upon, or place such a high value on the deceased that they will not grieve in order to avoid the reality of the loss."
- Reawakening of an old loss—"In some cases individuals are reluctant to grieve because the current loss reawakens a more profound and painful loss."
- Multiple losses—"Those who experience multiple losses such as the death of an entire family or a number of sequential losses within a relatively short period of time, sometimes have difficulty grieving because the losses are overwhelming to contemplate and deal with."

---

[101] Rando, *Grief, Dying, and Death*, 64-65.

- Inadequate ego development—"Such individuals are not psychologically able to successfully master the tasks of grief. Instead they frequently experience feelings of intense hopelessness, rage, frustration, depression, anxiety, and despair that they cannot defend against."
- Idiosyncratic resistances to mourning—"These are individuals who do not permit themselves to grieve because of specific psychological issues that interfere with the process. For example, some people will not grieve for fear of losing control or appearing weak to themselves and others."

B. *Social Factors in Unresolved Grief* [102]
- Social negation of a loss—"In this situation the loss is not socially defined as a loss, e.g., an abortion, a miscarriage, an infant given up for adoption. Although grief work is necessary, the social support for it is inadequate or nonexistent."
- Socially unspeakable loss—"In this case the loss is so 'unspeakable' that members of the social system cannot be of any assistance to the bereaved. Examples of such loss include death by an overdose of morphine, murder, suicide, or the death of an illicit lover." This is what Doka calls "disenfranchised grief."
- Social isolation and/or geographic distance from social support—"In this instance the individual is either away from her social supports at the time of mourning or there are no existing social supports available for assistance."
- Assumption of the role of the strong one—"In some situations there are certain people who are designated to be the 'strong one' by those around them."
- Uncertainty over the loss—"In cases where the loss is uncertain, such as when a boater is lost at sea or a child is kidnapped, the grievers and their social systems are often unable to commence grieving until they know the precise status of the lost person."

What Are Some Common Grief Avoidance Response Styles?

- According to Alan D. Wolfelt, there are some common grief avoidance response styles that are common patterns often adopted by those who have unresolved grief. Wolfelt identifies the avoidance patterns.[103]
  - The postponer—"The postponer is the person who believes that if you delay the expression of your grief over time it will hopefully go away."

---

[102] Rando, *Grief, Dying, and Death*, 66-67.
[103] Wolfelt, *Death and Grief*, 115-118.

o The displacer—"The displacer is the person who takes the expression of the grief away from the loss itself and displaces the feelings in other directions."

o The replacer—"The replacer is the person who takes the emotions that were invested in the relationship that ended in death and reinvests the emotions prematurely in another relationship."

o The minimizer—"The minimizer is the person who is aware of feelings of grief, but when felt, works to minimize the feelings by diluting them through a variety of rationalizations."

o The somaticizer—"The somaticizer is the person who converts his or her feelings of grief into physical symptoms."

What Factors Influence a Person's Individual Response to Loss?

- In studying the uniqueness of grief response, Alan D. Wolfelt suggests ten factors that influence grief that determines whether a person's grief will be normal or complicated.[104]

  o The nature of the relationship with the person who died—Different people will have different responses to loss based on the nature of the relationship. Intimate relationships and ambivalent relationships often interfere with a person's ability to cope with his or her losses.

  o The availability, helpfulness, and ability of the person to make use of a social support system—Whether or not the bereaved has a support network also affects the ability of the bereaved to cope with his or her loss.

  o The unique characteristics of the bereaved person—The individual characteristics of the bereaved often add to the complications of grief.

  o The unique characteristics of the person who died—Individual attributes of the deceased often add to the complications of grief. These characteristics can be positive or negative.

  o The nature of the death—Circumstances surrounding the death of a loved one have a tremendous impact on a survivor's grief. The age of the deceased, the suddenness of the loss, or the possibility of preventing the death all affect the bereaved's ability to cope with the loss.

  o The person's religious and cultural history—Different cultures are known for the ways they express or repress grief. Religious differences also assist or detract from a person's journey toward reconciliation of the loss.

---

[104] Wolfelt, *Death and Grief*, 26-31.

- o Other crises or stresses in the person's life—The secondary losses that come with grief often add to the complication of grief. In losing a spouse, there is also the loss of financial income, the loss of a close friend, and the potential loss of one's community.
- o Previous experiences with death—Prior negative associations with death can influence one's capacity to grieve in a healthy way.
- o The social expectations based on the sex of the survivor—Societal roles affect how individuals react to loss based on social conditioning. Males are taught to be strong, while females are expected to be emotional. These role expectations can lead to unresolved grief.
- o The ritual or funeral experience—The funeral experience serves to help the bereaved accept the loss. If the purpose of the funeral is minimized or distorted in some way, the experience of reconciling one's grief often becomes more difficult.

How Might We Diagnose Someone with Unresolved/Complicated Grief?

In studying complicated grief, J. William Worden identified twelve clues to diagnosing complicated grief.[105]

- Clue 1: The person being interviewed cannot speak of the deceased without experiencing intense and fresh grief.
- Clue 2: Some relatively minor event triggers an intense grief reaction.
- Clue 3: Themes of loss come up in a clinical interview.
- Clue 4: The person who has sustained the loss is unwilling to move material possessions belonging to the deceased.
- Clue 5: An examination of a person's medical record reveals that he or she has developed physical symptoms like those the deceased experienced before death.
- Clue 6: Those who make radical changes to their lifestyles following a death or who exclude from their life friends, family members, and/or activities associated with the deceased may be revealing unresolved grief.
- Clue 7: A patient presents a long history of subclinical depression, often marked by persistent guilt and lowered self-esteem.
- Clue 8: A compulsion to imitate the dead person, particularly if the client has no conscious desire or competence for the same behavior.

---

[105] Worden, *Grief Counseling*, 5th ed., 150-152.

- Clue 9: Although self-destructive impulses can be stimulated by a number of situations, unresolved grief can be one of these and should be considered.
- Clue 10: Unaccountable sadness occurring at a certain time each year can also be a clue to unresolved grief.
- Clue 11: A phobia about illness or death is often related to the specific illness that took the deceased.
- Clue 12: A knowledge of the circumstances surrounding the death can help the therapist determine the possibility of unresolved grief.

Potential Danger Signals in Grief Reactions

Charles Bachmann lists potential danger signals in grief reactions.[106]

- When the bereaved feels he or she is no longer of value as a person.
- When the bereaved acts in a manner inconsistent with his or her usual behavior.
- When the bereaved makes veiled threats at self-destruction.
- When the bereaved makes dramatic gestures through superficial attempts.
- When the bereaved exhibits antisocial behavior.
- When the bereaved demonstrates excessive hostility.
- When the bereaved engages in excessive drinking.
- When the bereaved is extremely moody.
- When the bereaved withdraws completely and no longer interacts with others.
- When the bereaved is fleeing reality by sudden decisions to fly to remote places.

For Reflection and Discussion

- In studying the theoretical foundations of unresolved grief, it is important to assess your own grief.
  - o Do you have any concerns about your own grief process?
  - o Are there potentially unresolved issues in your journey of grief that might hinder you in helping others with their grief?
- Students should complete a self-assessed grief timeline, acknowledging possible areas of unresolved grief in their own lives.
- Two excellent resources for this purpose:

---

[106] Bachmann, *Ministering to the Grief Sufferer*, 55-56.

1. *The Loss History Graph* by John W. James and Russell Friedman
2. *The Timeline Test* by June Hunt

The Timeline Test

Repressed grief can be overcome, and grieving can begin when a person takes "The Timeline Test." [107]

I.   **Draw** a long, horizontal line representing your life.
II.   **Divide** the timeline into three sections – childhood, youth, and adulthood.
III. **Denote** major changes in your life:

birth of siblings	*change of school*	*death of a loved one*
death of a pet	*lost friendships*	*abuse (verbal, emotional, physical)*
broken engagements	*abortion*	*marriage*
relocation	*miscarriage*	*childlessness, infertility*
"empty nest"	*separation/divorce*	*job loss/new job*
illnesses/injuries	*financial loss*	*retirement*

IV.   **Draw** short lines extending from the timeline and write short phrases by each line that describe all significant events.
V.   **Determine** whether there are any sad experiences or significant losses and hurts over which you have never grieved or have never finished grieving.
VI.   **Discover** the source of your masked pain through earnest prayer.
VII. **Define** the painful events over which you need to grieve by using specific statements.
    a. "I am grieving over…"
    b. "I felt abandoned by…"
    c. "I was really hurt when…"
VIII. **Decide** now to allow deep genuine grieving over your losses. (Jeremiah 17:14)
IX.   **Defuse** the power these events have over your emotions by sharing your feelings over your emotions and share your feelings with a trusted friend and with God. (Ecclesiastes 3:1,7)
X.   **Deepen** your dependence on the Lord to set you emotionally free. (Psalm 118:5)

---

[107] June Hunt, Grief: Living At Peace with Loss, (Torrance, CA: Rose Publishing,/Aspire Press, 2015), 14-16.

Session Three

Essential Grief Ministry Skills

Grief Ministry Skills in the Field of Bereavement/Grief

A. *What Is a Skill?*
- In its most basic definition, a skill is "the ability to do something well."[108]
- According to Tim Peterson and David Van Fleet, a skill is "the ability to perform some specific behavioral task or the ability to perform some specific cognitive process that is functionally related to some particular task."[109]
- In their work, Peterson and Van Fleet identify three components to skills.[110]
  1. a domain-specific knowledge base
  2. the means to access that knowledge
  3. the ability to take actions or thoughts using the knowledge to carry out a task
- The purpose of this project is to provide a domain-specific knowledge from the field of grief ministry that will equip participants with grief ministry skills that will enable them to become better ministers to the grieving.

---

[108] The Free Dictionary, s.v. "skill," accessed September 18, 2018, https://www.thefree dictionary.com/skill.

[109] Tim O. Peterson and David D. Van Fleet, "The Ongoing Legacy of R.L. Katz: An Updated Typology of Management Skills," *Management Decision* 42, no. 10 (2004): 1298.

[110] Peterson and Van Fleet, "Ongoing Legacy of R.L. Katz," 1298.

B. *What Are Soft Skills?*
- In the field of management, there are certain skills that are necessary for employment opportunities. Skills may be separated into "hard" skills and "soft" skills.
- Hard skills are those skills that are technical in nature that can be learned and easily observed, quantifiable, and measured, while soft skills are non-technical in nature and often related to interpersonal skills, human relations skills and social skills. These skills are often hard to observe, quantify or measure.
- Soft skills are "personal attributes that enable someone to interact effectively and harmoniously with other people."[111]
- The grief ministry skills identified by the project director are soft skills that the workshop participants may already possess, and yet with knowledge and practice can be enhanced.
- In acknowledging the grief ministry skills as soft skills, the facilitator fills the need to address a question that might come from an examination of the list, "Are these qualities of good grief sharers or are they actual skills to be learned and equipped?" The answer is "Yes!" They are both! They are qualities of good grief sharers and are skills to be enhanced. For example, empathy - some people are by their nature more empathetic than others, which would make them good grief sharers. It is the belief of the author that those who are less empathetic can improve their grief ministry skills in this area of ministry.
- It is the desire of the facilitator to equip the participants through education, and practice of the abovementioned skills.

C. *Are These Soft Skills Recognized by Both the Secular and Spiritual Fields?*
- The list of specific grief ministry skills is a result of the project director's research of both secular and Christian researchers and authors.
- According to Dr. Kenneth Doka, there "are six basic human needs relating to death: spiritual, financial, physical, cultural/ethnic, psychological, and social."[112] With this in mind, we have an immense opportunity to minister to individuals, each with multiple needs arising out of their experience of loss and grief.
- In the author's research, twenty grief ministry skills have been identified that are essential to equipping the participant's ministry to the grieving.
- Biblical support for these grief ministry skills will be addressed in session five through a case study from the book of Job.

---

[111] Dictionary.com, s.v. "soft skills," accessed September 18, 2018, https://www.dictionary.com /browse/soft-skills?s=t.
[112] Kenneth Doka, *Living with Grief After Sudden Loss* (Washington, DC: Hospice Foundation of America, 1996), 129.

- The twenty grief ministry skills identified by the project director are not all encompassing. There are many skills of lesser consideration that are nonetheless important. Additionally, some of the grief ministry skills are lightly examined, such as care, love, and mercy. Volumes have been written on these specific topics but minimally addressed in this project due to limited research on these qualities in the secular field. Though the facilitator gives them light treatment due to the lack of support in the secular study of grief, the biblical support for these qualities is overwhelming.
- With the purpose of this project blending the secular and the spiritual, the author gives more attention to the skills identified by the secular authors that have biblical support.

What Are the Primary and Secondary Skills of Grief Ministry?

Primary Grief Ministry Skills

Companioning—One of the most important grief ministry skills is that of companioning the grief sufferer. A companion walks alongside the grief sufferer during his or her time of mourning and readjustment. While a companion cannot do bereaved people's grief for them, neither should anyone "walk alone through the valley of the shadow of death."[113] According to Harold Ivan Smith, "Grief care is an opportunity to be a companion on the path, a companion through rough times, a companion in the daily struggle of grief. One of the most significant things you can ever do is to be a grief companion."[114] As Smith states about companioning, "Show up, sit down and stay a while."[115]

Companioning requires a commitment from the bereaved as well as the companion. Grief sufferers must allow someone to help them through their grief. This is not easily accomplished in a culture of individualism, with many people isolating themselves and refusing to allow people into their personal struggles. This individualism and isolationism makes it difficult to invite others to walk through it with you. To grief sufferers, it is a matter of trust and whether or not they are open to allow companioning as part of their grief work. Often grief sufferers feel that they must go it alone and save potential companions from the pain of their grief. Whatever the situation, it requires a commitment from the grief sufferers to allow someone

---

[113] Williams and Sturzl, *Grief Ministry,* 14.
[114] Smith, *When You Don't Know What to Say,* 15.
[115] Smith, *When You Don't Know What to Say,* 16.

to companion them through their time of grieving. As Norman H. Wright states, "Through grief you express your feelings about your loss. And you invited others to walk through it with you."[116]

For the companion, there must be a commitment to be available to the grief sufferer, without trying to fix the grief sufferer. According to Harold Ivan Smith, "You cannot do your friend's grief for them. You are not called to supervise or critique that person's grief. You, however, are called to witness this person's courageous efforts to come to terms with the loss."[117] Furthermore, Smith states, "Grief sharing is not about fixing ... it's about showing up."[118] According to noted author Alan Wolfelt, "Companioning the bereaved is not about assessing, analyzing, fixing, or resolving another's grief. Instead, it is about being totally present to the mourner, even being a temporary guardian of her soul."[119]

In his work, *The Handbook for Companioning the Mourner*, Alan D. Wolfelt outlines eleven tenets of companioning.[120]

✦ Tenet 1: Companioning is about being present to another person's pain; it is not about taking away the pain.

✦ Tenet 2: Companioning is about going to the wilderness of the soul with another human being; it is not about thinking you are responsible for finding the way out.

✦ Tenet 3: Companioning is about honoring the spirit; it is not about focusing on the intellect.

✦ Tenet 4: Companioning is about listening with the heart; it is not about analyzing with the head.

✦ Tenet 5: Companioning is about bearing witness to the struggles of others; it is not about judging or directing these struggles.

✦ Tenet 6: Companioning is about walking alongside; it is not about leading.

✦ Tenet 7: Companioning means discovering the gifts of sacred silence; it does not mean filling up every moment with words.

✦ Tenet 8: Companioning is about being still; it is not about frantic movement forward.

✦ Tenet 9: Companioning is about respecting disorder and confusion; it is not about imposing order and logic.

---

[116] Wright, *Reflections of a Grieving Spouse*, 41.
[117] Smith, *When You Don't Know What to Say*, 15.
[118] Wright, *Reflections of a Grieving Spouse*, 17.
[119] Alan Wolfelt, *The Handbook for Companioning the Mourner* (Fort Collins, CO: Companion Press, 2009), 3.
[120] Wolfelt, *Handbook for Companioning*, 13-104.

- ✦ Tenet 10: Companioning is about learning from others; it is not about teaching them.
- ✦ Tenet 11: Companioning is about curiosity; it is not about expertise. "Curiosity for the companion is about being willing to enter into and learn about the mystery of grief while recognizing you do not and cannot fully understand someone else's experience."

Empathy—While expressions of sympathy are appreciated by grief sufferers, the caregivers to the grief sufferers are better able to minister to them if they can empathize with their suffering. Norman Autton believes "Many who have themselves endured the pangs of grief and sorrow are of course the more able to enter into fullest sympathy and closest understanding of those who mourn."[121] The essential task of the minister is the "sharing of the person's grief."[122]

According to Williams and Sturzel, "Empathy is the ability to feel what another is feeling without losing yourself in the other's pain. You really share the other person's experience, but you remain yourself. Empathy implies acceptance and support."[123]

Alan Wolfelt feels that "Sympathy is a feeling of concern for someone else without necessarily becoming involved in a close, helping relationship; it projects an 'I feel sorry for you' attitude, but stops short of empathy." He further states that "active empathy is experienced when the mourner feels you understand" and that empathy "is communicated when you, the companion, respond at the emotional, feeling level of the mourner."[124]

Sharing in another person's pain is best accomplished through empathy. As Charles Bachmann states, "The sufferer needs those who will listen with deep abiding concern, who will empathize, which is much more than sympathize." He further explains, "To sympathize means to feel along with; to empathize means to feel into the situation of someone else in such a positive way that the individual knows that there is someone who walks with him, who knows the hurt and the painful reminders of days that used to be, who is standing by."[125]

According to Williams and Sturzel, "Both empathy and sympathy can evoke tears. Tears of sympathy flow because you feel sorry for the person in pain. Tears of empathy flow from actually feeling a small portion of that pain. In sympathy you are on the outside looking in; in empathy you have as the Native American says, 'crawled in through the person's feet up

---

[121] Norman Autton, *The Pastoral Care of the Bereaved* (London: William Clowes and Sons, Limited London and Beccles, 1967), 55.

[122] Tautges, *Comfort Those Who Grieve*, 110-111.

[123] Williams and Sturzl, *Grief Ministry*, 86.

[124] Wolfelt, *Handbook for Companioning*, 59-60.

[125] Bachmann, *Ministering to the Grief Sufferer*, 32.

through their belly, felt the pain in their chest, and are looking at the world through their eyes.'"[126]

Autton believes that empathy is "an active process of being there—to be able to go where the sufferer wants to go, to be able by standing there to communicate 'I understand,' without saying it in so many words."[127] Wolfelt states, "This dependable quality of empathy is what seems to free the mourner to open his heart and mourn from the inside out."[128] As Williams writes, "Usually people who feel called to be caregivers experience an element of 'feeling the pain of others' in their call. This feeling can propel the caring individual to share or lift the burden of those who are hurting." He believes that good comfort of the grief sufferer "requires empathy."[129]

According to Alan Wolfelt, there are four major benefits of empathy that bear witness without bringing judgment.[130]

+ Empathetic communication is a foundation upon which you establish a companion-witness relationship with the mourner.
+ The mourner who feels empathetically understood and not judged is more likely to risk sharing deep, soul-based encounters with grief.
+ The mourner's experience of your genuine effort and commitment to understand creates a trusting, low-threatening environment that negates the need for self-protection and isolation.
+ The communication of empathy encourages self-exploration in the mourner, a prerequisite for compassionate self-understanding and, eventually, movement toward reconciliation.

Gifting—Once a friend or loved one experiences grief, one of the easiest ways to express love and encouragement to the grief sufferer is that of a simple gift. According to author Brian Croft, "Everyone loves to receive gifts. Some appreciate them more than others, but most people whether they feel particularly loved by gifts or not appreciate the sentiment of the gift from the giver."[131] Gifting during times of grief expresses a love and concern that goes beyond words.

According to Harold Ivan Smith, "Flowers have long been a social expression of condolence. Flowers communicate caring when a friend cannot express words."[132]

---

[126] Williams and Sturzl, *Grief Ministry*, 85.
[127] Norman Autton, *Pastoral Care*, 72.
[128] Wolfelt, *Handbook for Companioning*, 60.
[129] Williams and Sturzl, *Grief Ministry*, 13
[130] Wolfelt, *Handbook for Companioning*, 62.
[131] Brian Croft, *Caring for Widows* (Wheaton, IL: Crossway Books, 2015), 113.
[132] Harold Ivan Smith, *When You Don't Know What to Say* (Kansas City, KS: Beacon Hill Press, 2012), 74.

It is common for churches to purchase flowers to display their love and encouragement to the bereaved. Another common gift that has grown in popularity in recent years is the purchase of pottery in loving memory of the deceased. In working with hospice, I deliver small pieces of pottery to bereaved families, of which many express their thankfulness.

In addition to flowers and pottery, another gift for the bereaved that can be practical and helpful is a book on grief. In my roles as pastor and hospice chaplain, I distribute a small booklet written by Kenneth Doka titled *Life Beyond Loss* to bereaved families. There are numerous books on grief at online bookstores that are both meaningful and practical. Some of the books I recommend are *Experiencing Grief* by H. Norman Wright, *Good Grief* by Granger E. Westberg, and *Grief: Living at Peace with Loss* by June Hunt. These books are easy to read and give grief sufferers a glimpse of hope in the midst of their despair.

Another essential gift that cannot be overlooked is prepared food. This has long been a tradition in churches, as it has been seen as a common expression of love. It is not unusual for church members to prepare meals for bereaved families before or after a funeral service. Furthermore, it is common to deliver food items to the homes of grieving families. The need to eat still exists within the grief sufferer's home, but preparing meals is exhausting and they often have no energy left for this task. The gift of a covered dish or a sandwich tray often brings relief to the grief sufferer as they are relieved of the added burden of preparing meals. The gifting of prepared meals can be a great blessing and is very appreciated.

Not to be overlooked in the skill of gifting is the simple card or personal note. According to Harold Ivan Smith, a card conveys, "(1) We love you. (2) We care. (3) Turn your heart toward Jesus." In sending a card as an expression of grief care, the sender wants to reassure the bereaved that he or she has "the sender's deepest, heartfelt, sincere, understanding sympathy for the loss."[133] Cards are sent with the hope that they will bring comfort to the bereaved as they realize that the grief sharer loves them and is praying for them in their time of loss. For the bereaved, a simple card is a reminder that someone cares.

Listening—In James 1:19, James wrote, "Let every man be swift to hear, slow to speak" (KJV). In the present culture, listening is a lost art. It is common for people to talk, but very few people actually know how to listen. When it comes to ministering to the grieving, "sympathetic listening will always help to release grief."[134] The grief sufferer "needs those who will listen with deep and abiding concern, who will empathize, which is more than sympathize." Ultimately, "listening is sharing a burden."[135]

---

[133] Smith, *When You Don't Know What to Say*, 70-71.
[134] Norman Autton, *Pastoral Care*, 60.
[135] Bachmann, *Ministering to the Grief Sufferer*, 32-37.

Harold Ivan Smith, in his study on grief, uses James Miller's quote from *The Art of Healing Presence* when he states, "There are three things you can do to help someone. The first is to listen, the second is to listen. The third is to listen more." Victoria Alexander states in her work with grief sufferers that "every griever has three essential needs: to find words to express the loss, to say the words aloud, and to know the words have been heard."[136]

For the caregiver, "providing the listening ear may be all that is necessary in order for the healing process to begin." In ministering to grieving people, "you can recognize that the words of the grief sufferer are an invitation for you to stop and listen."[137] The ability to listen is essential to minister to the grieving, and ultimately, to "listen attentively to another person is to lay down your life for that person."[138]

Often when a person tries to attend to the needs of a grief sufferer, he or she is trying to figure out what to say. Listening is the key to knowing what to say. Thomas Oden, in his book *Pastoral Theology*, states, "We learn what to say, in part, by listening to what is being said. If we let the person tell us where he or she is, we will soon learn how best to respond."[139]

The competent caregiver "takes time to really listen to the whole message—both the words and all the possible meanings behind them. It is especially important to search for feelings that the speaker may be expressing only indirectly because it is to these feelings that caregivers can most effectively respond." When listening to the grief sufferer, it is essential that the caregiver "listen for the feelings behind the words."[140]

In his work, Bachmann identifies two types of listening: disciplined listening and responsive listening. Disciplined listening is "listening to encourage others to talk," while responsive listening is to listen to "what the person says, hearing the meaning behind the words, catching nuance and overtones." According to Bachmann, when the caregiver "listens permissively, he opens the way for the grief sufferer to tell his story and develop his own insights as quickly as possible."[141]

A caregiver's task is to listen, stay with, and reassure the grief sufferer that what he or she is experiencing is normal. In his ministry to senior adult widows, Brian Croft states that one of the most important lessons is the "discipline to listen and learn." Croft purports that "[w]idows most need a patient, listening ear, together with sympathy and wise, sensitive

---

[136] Smith, *When You Don't Know What to Say*, 17-57.
[137] Smith, *When You Don't Know What to Say*, 41-42, 94.
[138] Williams and Sturzl, *Grief Ministry*, 69.
[139] Smith, *When You Don't Know What to Say*, 11.
[140] Williams and Sturzl, *Grief Ministry*, 81-82.
[141] Bachmann, *Ministering to the Grief Sufferer*, 37.

counsel."[142] Alan Wolfelt, in his study on companioning, states, "companions are hospitality hosts who patiently listen to love stories."[143]

According to Williams and Sturzl, "listening skills can be learned, but they are more than mechanical techniques. They are, in fact, the enfleshment of your love, care, and empathy for others."[144]

Prayer—One of the greatest opportunities to minister to grief sufferers comes in our willingness to pray for and with them. It is common in our expressions of sympathy to express our continued prayers for the grief sufferer. According to Harold Ivan Smith, "a helper prays for the grieving, and a helper prays with the grieving." Smith further notes, "In grief, few are experts at praying. We are all beginners and bunglers, groping in our emotional darkness for words."[145]

In his work with widows, Brian Croft states that caregivers "best accomplish spiritual care through prayer and the ministry of the Word that intentionally focused on God's desire and care for widows." Croft says it is important that "when you pray, pray specific biblical truths." Croft suggests praying through these biblical truths.[146]

- *Praise* God for His sovereign power over death and the pain of separation from our loved ones.
- *Thank* God for the hope we have of resurrection one day because of Christ, even in the face of deep loss.
- *Exalt* our Savior Jesus Christ who ministers grace and mercy in our greatest times of need.
- *Rejoice* in the promise of God that He will never leave us or forsake us and that it extends to even the loneliest of widows.

In my time as a pastor and hospice chaplain, the goal is to have prayer with every person and their families. In praying for those who have experienced the loss of loved ones eternally prepared, I pray specifically for three things for the family:

- Pray that the family can feel the presence of the Lord, knowing He will never leave them or forsake them.

---

[142] Croft, *Caring for Widows*, 17, 103.

[143] Wolfelt, *The Handbook for Companioning*, 7.

[144] Williams and Sturzl, *Grief Ministry*, 70.

[145] Smith, *When You Don't Know What to Say*, 81.

[146] Croft, *Caring for Widows*, 81-88, 93.

✦ Pray that the Lord would comfort their hearts and minds in Christ Jesus as only He can.

✦ Pray that the Lord would provide them strength to endure the loss.

To close the prayer, specifically thank God for their friendship, their family, and their faith in Jesus Christ as Lord and Savior.

Presence—In the list of essential grief ministry skills, near the top is "presence." Presence is simply being present in the life of the grief sufferer, as "no one should walk alone through the valley of the shadow of death."[147] Presence is as simple as "show up, sit down, and stay a while."[148] Smith acknowledges, "Through your presence, you can make a difference—even when you don't know what to say or do."[149]

Individuals often neglect visiting the bereaved because they do not know what to say, thus leaving the grief sufferers alone in their grief. This should not be! According to Williams and Sturzl, "What you say is not nearly as important as your presence."[150] Autton agrees that "by our mere physical presence with a sorrowing family we shall offer strength and support."[151]

It is comforting to the grief sufferer to know "there is someone who walks with him, who knows the hurt and the painful reminders of days that used to be, who is standing by."[152] Ultimately, the person who is present in the grief sufferer's life will "communicate the idea that someone cares."[153]

Individuals who commit to being present to another person's grief become healing forces in the grief sufferer's life. Smith says, "sitting alone in shared silence can be healing for both the griever and the helper."[154] Williams and Sturzl state, "being in the presence of someone who is honest and true, enables those who mourn to enter into their own truth."[155] Bachmann says, "practicing the presence of quietness in bearing and attitude creates the atmosphere in which another can begin to unburden himself."[156]

Furthermore, Williams and Sturzl state, "As a caregiver, your task is to listen, abide with, and assure the grieving person that these experiences are normal and with time will

---

[147] Smith, 14.
[148] Smith, 16.
[149] Smith, *When You Don't Know What to Say*, 14-16.
[150] Williams and Sturzl, *Grief Ministry*, 75.
[151] Autton, *Pastoral Care*, 59.
[152] Bachmann, 92.
[153] Bachmann, *Ministering to the Grief Sufferer*, 92.
[154] Smith, *When You Don't Know What to Say*, 49.
[155] Williams and Sturzl, *Grief Ministry*, 90.
[156] Bachmann, *Ministering to the Grief Sufferer*, 33.

abate."[157] To be present to another person's pain is a healing force of its own. When the grief sufferer recognizes that you are there to support him or her in the midst of his or her pain, this reinforces your care and concern.

As Christians, we as caregivers are also "privileged to be a sign to them (the grief sufferer) of God's presence." When we come alongside the grief sufferer, we "symbolize the spirit of Him who came to comfort and to heal broken relationships." We represent the very presence of Christ. As Bachmann states of the Christian caregiver, "The pastor (or any Christian) can communicate the concern of God whom he serves, the Church he represents, and the community in which he works. He can, by his presence, symbolize that profound hope which is not always verbalized—that God does not forsake His children."[158] Furthermore, Williams states, "As a caregiver you are privileged to be a sign to them of God's presence."[159]

In equipping the church, it is essential that the church understands that sharing in another's grief is "kingdom work." The church needs to understand that it has a calling to be equipped and "through the power of the Comforter, make a difference in the lives of the bereaving." Thus, grief sharing is an opportunity "to partner with God in fulfilling the beatitude—'Blessed are those who mourn, for they will be comforted by God through people like you.'"[160]

Scripture—One of the greatest comforts to Christians is a timely read Scripture passage in the middle of their sorrow. Though this is normally reserved for pastors, the reading of Scripture can be used by all Christians as a comfort measure in times of grief. Williams states, "The Word of God nourishes, enlivens, and calls you forth in ministry."[161] Brian Croft states of Christian ministry that ministers "best accomplish spiritual care through prayer and the ministry of the Word that is intentionally focused on God's desire and care."[162] This may seem overly simplified, but the Christian caregiver to grieving souls should not forget or neglect the Word of God in comforting the bereaved.

The Holy Scriptures are an indispensable part of my work with the grieving, both in my work of the church and as a hospice chaplain. The most frequently used passages are Psalm 23, Psalm 46, Psalm 121, Matthew 5:4, John 14:1-3, Hebrews 13:5, and Revelation 21:4-6, though there are many more that can be used by the minister and layman to comfort the bereaved.

---

[157] Williams and Sturzl, *Grief Ministry*, 35.
[158] Bachmann, *Ministering to the Grief Sufferer*, 25.
[159] Williams and Sturzl, *Grief Ministry*, 111.
[160] Williams and Sturzl, *Grief Ministry*, 107.
[161] Williams and Struzl, *Grief Ministry*, 107.
[162] Croft, *Caring for Widows*, 88.

Sensitivity—One of the greatest needs for individuals working with grief sufferers is to be sensitive. Death and grief often expose the raw emotions of the grief sufferer, and as a result, the grief sufferer cannot fully control his or her actions. Those ministering to the grief sufferer must be sensitive to his or her needs. As Bachmann states, "If the pastor (or caregiver) has a real sensitivity to the needs of others he will be, or will become, aware of how his presence or person may be utilized to the best advantage."[163] Jon Joyce states, "Whatever you as pastor or congregation as the family of God determine to do, be sure that you are being sensitive to the individual needs of the persons involved." In addition, Joyce believes that we need to "Be sensitive to the needs of each individual and plan the remainder of your follow up that way."[164]

Being sensitive often means being aware of the various needs of the bereaved, whether emotional or physical. As a caregiver, you must try to be sensitive about probing. According to Williams and Sturzl, "Probing for facts is not helpful. Probing in order to help people talk and clarify their own experience, on the other hand, is helpful."[165] In his book, *Comfort Those Who Grieve: Ministering God's Grace in Times of Loss*, Paul Tautges suggests a five-step process in which being sensitive is a necessity.[166]

+ First, establish understanding with a tender touch and a few nonintrusive questions to determine immediate needs, discerning any immediate needs or fears.
+ Second, show compassion by empathizing with the person's pain, being sensitive to immediate needs, and always speaking graciously.
+ Third, obtain permission to help where help is needed by gently asking for permission without being bombastic.
+ Fourth, dispense biblical comfort and hope with appropriate Scriptures and offer to pray with the person.
+ Fifth, give the person assurance of your continued prayers and support.

It is essential for the caregiver to be sensitive during the grieving process, but the acute phase of grief is the most volatile time. It is when the grief sufferer is vulnerable to the raw emotions that surface. This is when it is most important to "listen to the heart (of the grief sufferer) to hear what is behind the person's words (fear, worry, doubt, etc.). Ask the Holy Spirit to make you sensitive."[167] Sensitivity at this vital time is crucial and will determine the

---

[163] Bachmann, *Ministering to the Grief Sufferer*, 36-37.

[164] Jon L. Joyce, *The Pastor and Grief* (Lima, OH: C.S.S. Publishing Co., Inc.), 127-129.

[165] Williams and Sturzl, *Grief Ministry*, 89.

[166] Tautges, *Comfort Those Who Grieve*, 110-111.

[167] Tautges, *Comfort Those Who Grieve*, 110.

effectiveness of your ministry to the grieving. Insensitivity at this vital time can have negative consequences for all involved and will limit a person's ability to minister to the grief sufferer.

Secondary Grief Ministry Skills

Acceptance—One of the most basic of needs of those suffering grief is the need for acceptance. According to Autton, "the majority (of grief sufferers) will need to express their emotions, and they must be prepared and helped to express as much grief as they will feel."[168] Bachmann says to "accept the person where he is."[169] In our grief-aversive society, much social pressure is placed on those who suffer a loss to keep their grief to a minimum. It is as though one can grieve too long and thus make others uncomfortable. It is as though there is a socially acceptable timeframe for grief and if you go beyond it you have committed social injustice. There is no grief time limit, and to expect the grief sufferer to meet socially preconceived expectations for his or her grief is unfair to that person. Thus, accepting grief sufferers where they are offers them a safe place to share their experiences. If they do not feel their grief is welcome, they will not feel welcome themselves. Acceptance is important to a grief sufferer's healing and resolution.

Acts of Kindness—Another basic need of the grief sufferer is simple acts of kindness. Often after a loss, those who are grieving are in shock and limited in their ability to do some of the simplest of things. If a grief sufferer is open to you being in his or her home, performing simple household chores can be of great value. Simple acts of sweeping the floors, helping with laundry, washing dishes, or even running errands can be extremely helpful. Additionally, some grief suffers, especially widows, are in need of simple maintenance around their homes, such as raking leaves, cleaning gutters, providing rides, changing light bulbs, or fixing something.[170] These simple acts of kindness can be great ministry opportunities for deacons, men's ministries, family ministries, or even youth groups. For a senior adult on a fixed income, these simple acts of kindness are extremely beneficial.

Awareness—When ministering to the grief sufferer, it is often essential "to do some advanced investigating about the people and their situation. Through this investigation, you may become aware of some issues."[171] It is important that the minister learn as much as possible about the grief sufferer and his or her situation as the minister tries to meet his or her basic needs. The

---

[168] Autton, *Pastoral Care*, 56.
[169] Bachmann, *Ministering to the Grief Sufferer*, 38.
[170] Croft, *Caring for Widows*, 115.
[171] Williams and Sturzl, *Grief Ministry*, 75.

need for awareness does not mean that the helper has the right to be intrusive and infringe on the personal life of the grief suffer. It merely means that the helper needs to be aware of pertinent information that will help him or her minister to the physical, social, emotional, and spiritual needs of the bereaved. The helper must be informed in order to achieve this. A grief helper cannot attend to the needs of a grief sufferer if he or she is not aware of the need.

Care—The basis of all grief ministry is an attitude of caring. Grief sufferers need people in their lives that truly care about them in their time of grief. Sharing in someone's grief "looks for an opportunity to actively care."[172] Throughout the history of Christianity, "Christians have not sprinted away in the face of pain. Early believers not only cared for the grieving but also buried the dead. Christians graciously washed and laid out the body, wove shrouds, gathered flowers, dug the grave, carried the corpse and fed the bereaved."[173] Though much has changed in contemporary society, a death event is still an excellent opportunity to show others that we care. You will see "God's glory displayed in his people caring for those in need for the sake of the gospel."[174] Much more could be said about "care," but that is fleshed out in other grief ministry skills, including empathy, gifting, listening, and presence.

Comfort—Comforting the bereaved is an opportunity to partner with God in fulfilling this beatitude: "Blessed are those who mourn, for they shall be comforted" (Matt. 5:4 NKJV). According to Warren Wiersbe, "The English Word 'comfort' comes from two Latin words that mean 'with strength.'"[175] In partnering with God, we are to offer genuine help and comfort to those who have lost loved ones. As Harold Ivan Smith states, "We are called. We are equipped. We can, through power of the Comforter, make a difference in the lives of the bereaving." To genuinely provide comfort to the bereaved, comforters must "be prepared to let the pain of another become their own and so let it transform them."[176] Like care, comfort is carried out in a number of other soft skills, such as presence and spiritual words.

According to Nancy Guthrie, author of *What Grieving People Wish You Knew About What Really Helps and What Really Hurts*, there are several things that can be done to comfort families.[177]

---

[172] Smith, *When You Don't Know What to Say*, 17.

[173] Smith, *When You Don't Know What to Say*, 30.

[174] Croft, *Caring for Widows*, 115.

[175] Tautges, *Comfort Those Who Grieve*, 15.

[176] Smith, *When You Don't Know What to Say*, 13, 115.

[177] Nancy Guthrie, *What Grieving People Wish You Knew About What Really Helps and What Really Hurts* (Wheaton, IL: Crossway Publishing, 2016).

1. *Don't try to "fix" their grief, but do say something.* To people who have lost someone they love, it is as if a hurdle has been erected between them and everyone else until the loss is acknowledged in some way. They just want you to say something simple like, "I'm so sad with you." They want you to say *something.*

2. *Don't tell a story about your own or someone else's loss.* Keep the focus on the person who is grieving. We might think the story of our experience or someone else's will be helpful, but it won't be.

3. *Be a welcome companion in grief, regardless of how well you know them.* Sometimes we stay away from people going through grief because we think they must have closer friends who are coming alongside them during this hard time and that we would be an unwelcome intrusion.

4. *Give them permission to cry.* Sometimes we are afraid to bring up people's losses because we don't want to "make them sad" if it seems like they are having a good day. But they are *already* sad. Their grief is like a computer program always running in the background. If you ask about their grief or share how you have been thinking about the person who died and they begin to weep, it's not that you made them sad. You simply gave them an opportunity to release some of the sadness that was already there in the form of tears.

5. *Proactively meet practical needs.* Grieving people will not usually call you if they need something. What they really need is for people around them to figure out something that would be helpful and just do it. No one is ever going to call and ask someone to clean their toilets, wash their clothes, get groceries, or run other errands. But sometimes that is what they really need.

6. *Use their loved one's name in conversation.* The greatest fear grieving people have is that the person they love will be forgotten. The person is gone from their presence, and they're afraid that person will be erased from everyone's thoughts. To hear someone simply speak that person's name is like a balm to the soul of a grieving person.

7. *If you knew the person who died, tell his or her grieving loved one a story about him or her.* Grieving people long to hear specific stories about experiences others had with their loved one, stories that highlight specific qualities about the person and instances in which those qualities were evident. Stories like this bring joy in the midst of sorrow to a grieving person.

8. *If at all possible, simply show up at the visitation, the funeral, and beyond.* If you can't make it to the visitation or the funeral, don't tell the person why you couldn't come (unless you were on the other side of the world or in a coma). Whatever reason kept you from being there on the lowest day of their life, when they wanted the world to

stop and notice the person that they loved died, simply won't be good enough. Just say that you are disappointed you could not be there. Ask the person to tell you about aspects of the service that were special to them. Maybe even ask if you can come over and watch a video of the service with them.

9. *Invite them to talk about their grief and their loved one who died.* Many grieving people will feel judged on their emotional or spiritual health by their honest response. The ups and downs and waves of grief can overtake even the most emotionally and spiritually sound people. The best question to ask is, "What's your grief like these days?" By asking this question, you're acknowledging their sorrow, affirming the normalcy of such sadness, and allowing them to talk about it.

10. *Reach out to the grieving member of your congregation on the anniversary of their loved one's death.* There is a day that comes around every year for the person who has lost someone he or she loves. Every year, as that day draws near, there is a sense of dread. The grieving person is trying to figure out what to do with the day to honor the memory of the person who died. Sometimes, there's no energy for that and he or she is just trying to get through the day. Regardless of how much time has passed since a person's loved one died, it means the world for someone to care enough to send a note, make a call, invite him or her to share a meal, or offer to accompany him or her to the grave."[178]

Compassion—At the heart of grief ministry is the need for the very compassion that Christ had for the grief sufferer. On more than one occasion in the Bible, Jesus had compassion for those who had lost loved ones. One example is from Luke chapter 7; the widow from Nain had experienced the death of her only son. Luke 7:13 states of Jesus, "When the Lord saw her, He had compassion on her and said to her, 'Do not weep'" (NKJV). Jesus then proceeded to raise the woman's son from the dead and present him to his mother.

Showing compassion to those who mourn the loss of a loved one is the very essence of Christ in the believer. As Jesus was full of compassion, so should we. Brian Croft states, "Such compassion (as Jesus) and love ought to be freely, cheerfully, and willingly displayed."[179] In addition, Paul Tautges recommends that the primary goal of those who minister to the grieving is to "establish rapport by showing compassion."[180] Furthermore, Alan Wolfelt states that "before the advent of the specialist and the evolution of our mourning avoidant culture,

---

[178] Adapted from Guthrie, *What Grieving People Wish.*
[179] Croft, *Caring for Widows,* 26.
[180] Tautges, *Comfort Those Who Grieve,* 110.

people turned to their neighbors and friends for support and compassion."[181] Prior to the commercialization of funerals that is prominent in the modern culture, it was common for the church to show its compassion for fellow believers by helping with many aspects of the funeral. Fellow believers would build the coffin, prepare the body for burial, cut fresh flowers from their gardens, and stay with the bereaved family through the duration of the funeral. Compassion is truly at the heart of grief ministry, and the opportunity is great.

Helping—One of the most basic skills of grief ministry is that of the helper. As mentioned previously in this session, there are "six basic human needs relating to death: spiritual, financial, physical, cultural/ethnic, psychological, and social."[182] It is common for the grief sufferer to need assistance in one or more of these areas so that the grief sufferer can focus on his or her mourning. As Harold Ivan Smith states, "Blessed are those who show up and anticipate what needs to be done." He further states that "when a friend, neighbor, or loved one has died, one of the first gifts a helper can offer is to call the residence to volunteer immediate practical help."

This takes place in the form of washing dishes, minor housekeeping, and even laundry if the grief sufferer is comfortable with it. Grief and loss seldom happens at our convenience, and often the grief sufferer feels overwhelmed at the slightest of tasks. When someone is overwhelmed with grief, often simple tasks become complicated, and a little help from a close friend is highly valued.

Smith further states that "grief sharers ask three questions: What can I do? What can I not do? And what shall I do first?" Helping a friend in need can be as simple as offering to make calls to friends and relatives. Also, if there are young children in the home, they still have to be bathed, fed, and given attention. If company is to arrive in wake of the loss, oftentimes housekeeping duties increase. According to Smith, "Helpful acts free the primary griever to focus on active grieving."[183]

Love—It is both biblical and practical to minster to the grieving with love and mercy. In ministry to the bereaved, "the church is to demonstrate mercy and love."[184] To become a caregiver of the grief sufferer, "you become a loving and open person to the other and set aside your own agenda and expectations."[185] In essence, caring for grief sufferers demands sacrificial love, a love that puts others first above a person's own needs. There must be a

---

[181] Wolfelt, *The Handbook for Companioning*, 5-6

[182] Doka, *Living with Grief*, 129.

[183] Smith, *When You Don't Know What to Say*, 66-68.

[184] Croft, *Caring for Widows*, 141.

[185] Williams and Sturzl, *Grief Ministry*, 69.

"genuine love for another that is a non-possessive love that accepts others just as they are and desires the best for them."[186] It is important that the love of Christ flow through the caregiver to the grief sufferer to "make the love of God real to the person you visit." As Brian Croft states, "Such compassion (as Jesus) and love ought to be freely, cheerfully, and willingly displayed."[187] As with compassion and care, much more could be stated about "love," but we will see it fleshed out in other grief ministry skills, including empathy, gifting, listening, and presence.

Reassurance—Often in the midst of their grief, the bereaved struggle to think properly as the emotions consume them. It is during these times that caregivers have the opportunity to give calming reassurance to the grief sufferer. Primarily, calming reassurance will have two aspects: the normalcy of grief and the comforting presence of the Lord. As for the normalcy of grief, Williams states "as a caregiver, your task is to listen, abide with, and assure the grieving person that these experiences are normal and with time will abate."[188] The grief sufferer is consumed by the raw emotions of grief and often cannot distinguish between normalcy and lunacy. It is common, even in normal grief, for a grief sufferer to think he or she is going insane. The other aspect of reassurance is that it is possible "to reassure people of God's loving presence."[189] Paul Tautges states "to effectively minister God's grace in times of loss, we must remind ourselves of the comforting character and ministry of God. During the process of grieving, the people who are experiencing loss need a great deal of reassurance." Tautges suggests five reassurances that one can give grief sufferers.[190]

1. Reassure them that grieving is not a sin.
2. Reassure them of the character of God.
3. Reassure them through the ministry of your presence and prayers.
4. Reassure them of the need to let others serve them.
5. Reassure them that God will walk through the future with them.

Silence—According to Harold Ivan Smith, "sometimes ministering to others simply means being quiet."[191] The practice of silence is often one of the most overlooked grief ministry skills. Thus, silence can be one of the most important grief ministry skills. Essentially, to be silent is

---

[186] Williams and Sturzl, *Grief Ministry*, 89-90.
[187] Croft, *Caring for Widows*, page 29
[188] Williams and Sturzl, *Grief Ministry*, 69-90.
[189] Williams and Sturzl, *Grief Ministry*, 88.
[190] Tautges, *Comfort Those Who Grieve*, 114-115.
[191] Smith, *When You Don't Know What to Say*, 48.

to acknowledge "we cannot answer all the questions."[192] According to Bachmann, "practicing the presence of quietness in bearing and attitude creates the atmosphere in which another can begin to unburden himself."[193] The truth is that sometimes, "sitting alone in shared silence can be healing for both the griever and the helper."[194]

Practicing silence can be uncomfortable for caregivers, especially for those who love to talk or cannot stand the awkwardness that silence brings. In those periods of awkward silence, the caregiver is often tempted to start or carry a conversation. It is specifically at these times when the caregiver needs to limit his or her words because "there will be times when a grief sharer does not know what to say."[195]

Essentially, when you do not know what to say, it is important that you do not say the wrong things. The old proverb "silence is golden" is a good rule of thumb to practice when one does not know what to say.

According to Alan Wolfelt, silence is sacred, as it means "not filling up every moment with words." It allows the caregiver to be "fully present to another human being who doesn't really need your words but values your soulful presence." Wolfelt specifically encourages caregivers to "cherish silence and respect how vital it is to the healing journey."[196]

Sympathy—It is common to express sympathy toward those who have had a loved one die. To sympathize means to "feel along with."[197] We often attend funeral visitations or the funeral ceremonies or memorial services in order to display our sympathy. To be present at these special events displays our love and concern for the bereaved and respect for what the family is experiencing. Though not as personal and intimate as empathy, sympathy is a genuine way to express our condolences and show a genuine concern for the grief sufferer. Much has been addressed in the "empathy" section of this session.

Talking/Conversing—Though "silence is golden," often there is a need for the caregiver to speak with love and concern to the grief sufferer, knowing that "it is normal for the grief sufferer to want to talk about the deceased." To do this, one must be sensitive to the grief sufferer and carefully ask questions in a nonintrusive way. Two easily asked nonintrusive statements to initiate conversation are, "Would you like to talk about it?" or "Tell me how things are."[198]

---

192 Autton, *Pastoral Care*, 66.
193 Bachmann, *Ministering to the Grief Sufferer*, 33.
194 Smith, *When You Don't Know What to Say*, 49.
195 Smith, *When You Don't Know What to Say*, 105.
196 Wolfelt, *Handbook for Companioning*, 75-77.
197 Bachmann, *Ministering to the Grief Sufferer*, 32.
198 Bachmann, *Ministering to the Grief Sufferer*, 17, 31.

Even the experts admit that sometimes they do not know what to say. In the words of Harold Ivan Smith, "Sometimes I don't know what to say even though I am a grief educator. There are no experts on grief when it comes to composing words."[199] According to Thomas Oden, in his book *Pastoral Theology*, "We learn what to say, in part by listening to what is being said. If we let the person tell us where he or she is, we will soon learn how best to respond."[200]

One of the most common mistakes caregivers make in talking is that of using clichés. Harold Ivan Smith, in his book *What to Say When You Don't Know What to Say,* acknowledges the need to avoid using clichés and platitudes. Smith identifies four general categories of clichés: (1) the generic—"Time heals all wounds;" (2) the spiritual—"God never puts more on us than we can handle;" (3) the admonitions—"Be strong for your children;" and (4) the laudatory—"You're holding up so well."[201] When a person resorts to clichés, it is often because they don't know what to say but they want to say something.

If the grief sufferer is open to talking, one question the caregiver might ask is, "What should we talk about?" In his book, *Caring for Widows*, Brian Croft states that "topics such as how the widow is feeling, the family members caring for her, a typical day, history about her life, her testimony of conversion, marriage and child-rearing advice, and ways to pray for her are all great ways to carry a conversation."[202]

For Reflection and Discussion

- We divided the soft skills into primary and secondary skills.
  - Primary skills: companioning, empathy, gifting, listening, prayer, presence, scripture, and sensitivity.
  - Secondary skills: acceptance, acts of kindness, awareness, care, comfort, compassion, helping, love, reassurance, silence, sympathy, and talking/conversing.
- In examining the list of grief ministry skills, answer these questions:
  - What skills do you feel you have mastered?
  - What skill do you feel you most need to improve?

---

[199] Smith, *When You Don't Know What to Say*, 46.
[200] Smith, *When You don't Know What to Say*, 11.
[201] Smith, *When You Don't Know What to Say*, 47.
[202] Croft, *Caring for Widows*, 153.

Session Four

Development of Essential Grief Ministry Skills

A Case Study from the Life of Job: A Biblical Basis for Grief Ministry Skills

- The biblical basis for the aforementioned grief ministry skills can be easily supported using multiple scriptural references. Because of lack of time and space, I will limit the biblical support of ministering to the grieving to the book of Job in the Old Testament.
- In the story of Job, we see how he lost seven sons and three daughters in one tragic event and how his friends came to support him.
- Over a short period of time, Job lost his wealth, his health, and ten children.

A. Theoretical Application of Grief Principles

1. *What kinds of grief are evident in the life of Job?*
   a. Acute grief—This is the sudden overwhelming grief that comes upon a person at the loss of a loved one.
   b. Compound grief—This type of grief occurs when you have more than one loss at a time.

    c.   Conflicted grief—The grief reaction is associated with a previously dependent relationship. This loss is conflicted because it cannot be explained spiritually in Job's relationship with God.

    d.   Normal grief—The grief sufferer displays normal symptoms of grief.

    e.   Unanticipated grief—The event happened so suddenly that there was no time to anticipate his losses.

2.   *What are the normal grief symptoms exhibited by Job?*

    a.   Emotional symptoms: sadness, anger, fatigue, helplessness, shock, and numbness

    b.   Physical symptoms: muscle weakness and lack of energy

    c.   Cognitive symptoms: disbelief, confusion, and preoccupation

    d.   Behavioral symptoms: sleep disturbances, appetite disturbances, social withdrawal, and crying.

3.   *What stages or tasks of grief are evident in the life of Job?*

    a.   Elizabeth Kubler Ross's five stages:

        1.   Denial and isolation (shock)—From the beginning, Job is shocked over the wave of losses.

        2.   Anger—Job experiences anger with his friends and at times with God.

        3.   Bargaining—Job desires for God to take his life and answer him, and questions what God is doing without losing faith.

        4.   Depression—Job experiences hopelessness and depression.

        5.   Acceptance—Job reaches this stage only in the final chapter of the book.

    b.   Bowlby and Parkes's four phases of grief:

        1.   Phase of numbness—Job sits on the ground in silence!

        2.   Phase of yearning and searching—This phase continues throughout most of the book.

        3.   Phase of disorganization and despair—This phase continues throughout most of the book.

        4.   Phase of reorganization—Job reaches this phase only in the final chapters of the book.

    c.   J. William Worden's four tasks of grief:

        1.   To accept the reality of the loss—This was a difficult process for Job.

        2.   To experience the pain of grief—Job's pain is prominent throughout the book.

        3.   To adjust to an environment in which the deceased is missing—This is not mentioned, though it had to be present in his life.

4. To find a way to remember the deceased while embarking on the rest of one's journey through life—Eventually the Lord restores his health, his wealth, and gives him more children.

4. *Contemporary Theories of Grief*
   a. Attachment theory—The greater the bond, the greater the loss. Job loved his children, and for them to die in tragedy was an extreme detachment. To recover from the loss of ten children would create an almost unbearable time of mourning, even with a strong faith.
   b. Tasks of mourning—Job worked through his grief in great detail throughout the book, as he had difficulty accepting his losses and processing the pain. It was difficult for Job to adjust to a world without his children, particularly the spiritual crisis that was much of the focus of the whole book. Eventually Job was able to process his grief and experience renewed hope as God restored his health, wealth, and family.
   c. Continuing bonds—Little can be determined from the biblical account of Job's grief.
   d. Meaning reconstruction—Job searched for meaning and that meaning had to be reconstructed in the aftermath of the loss of all ten children. Job's life story changed, yet the Lord reconstructed his life after loss and blessed him anew.
   e. Dual process—Job's grief oscillated between loss and restoration, with much of the book focusing on him grieving his loss. It is only at the end of the book of Job that we see him move toward restoration.

B. Application of Grief Ministry Skills from the Story of Job

Primary Passage: Job 2:11-13 (NIV)

When Job's three friends, Eliphaz the Temanite, Bildad the Shuhite, Zophar the Naamathite, heard about all the troubles that had come upon him, they set out from their homes and met together by agreement to go and sympathize with him and comfort him. When they saw him from a distance, they could hardly recognize him, they began to weep aloud, and they tore their robes and sprinkled dust on their heads. Then they sat on the ground with him for seven days and seven nights. No one said a word to him, because they saw how great his suffering was.

Job experienced the loss of seven sons and three daughters! Additionally, he lost his wealth and eventually his health. Job suffered much loss, and great was his grief. After suffering the loss of his children, several friends came to minister to Job in this most difficult time. The following comments examine the grief ministry skills they used, as well as their mistakes, and takes a further look at the advantage we have through the lens of contemporary ministry. The story of Job will encompass the twenty-one grief ministry skills examined earlier, as well as additional useful skills when ministering to the grieving.

What they did right ...

1. *Companioning*—"When Job's three friends ...." Companioning is important in the midst of grief.
2. *Awareness*—They "heard about all the troubles that had come upon him." You can't do anything for someone if you are not aware of it.
3. *Prioritizing*—They "set out from their homes." Ministry to the grieving must be a priority!
4. *Availability*—They "met together by agreement to go." It took effort.
5. *Sympathy*—They went to "sympathize with him."
6. *Comfort*—They went to "comfort him."
7. *Empathy*—They "began to weep aloud, and they tore their clothes and sprinkled dust on their heads."
8. *Presence*—They "sat on the ground with him for seven days and seven nights."
9. *Silence*—"No one said a word to him because they saw how great his suffering was."
10. *Allowance for expression of feelings*—They let him talk! Encourage the grief sufferer to share his or her thoughts and feelings.
11. *Gifting*—At the end of the book of Job, his friends and family brought him gifts. Gifting during the time of Job was a proper display of affection and is still an essential part of grief ministry today.
12. *Care*—They cared for Job's needs.

What they tried to do, but it didn't work out very well ...

1. They offered what they thought were *encouraging words*.
   + They had the best intentions.
2. They shared *spiritual conversation*, trying to explain God's place in Job's suffering.
   + It was in the expression of their words that they failed miserably.
3. They offered *consolation*.
   + We really want to say the right thing, the comforting thing.
   + We want to express our condolences.

4. They offered their *"wise" counsel.*
    +   They tried offering the best wisdom that they had.
    +   They had served the Lord for many years and had gained a lot of wisdom, by their own measurement, but our best wisdom is limited in nature.
5. They tried to be "*healers.*"
    +   Those who minister to grief sufferers are in fact entering into an attempt to heal the grief sufferer.
6. They tried *helping.*
    +   We have the best intentions in helping those who have suffered loss.

What they did wrong …

1. They *accused* the grief sufferer of guilt.
    +   Often, those who have experienced great grief deal with guilt and have trouble getting beyond it. Even if guilt is justified, there is grace in the Lord. There is no need to try to be the Holy Spirit and convict the person of guilt. Besides, we know in part that we have limited knowledge. We do not know what God is doing or how He will use pain in our lives.
2. They *talked too much.*
    +   More than likely a person will not remember anything you say unless you say something wrong.
3. They were *judgmental* toward their friend.
    +   More than one of Job's friends accused Job of hidden sin that caused the disaster, yet God said Job was righteous in all His ways.
4. They did not offer *unconditional acceptance.*
    +   The one thing Job needed that they failed to offer was unconditional acceptance.
5. They tried offering *comforting spiritual words.*
    +   They thought they were wise enough to give Job spiritual advice, and they offered their limited opinion with confidence and painful consequences.

What they lacked …

1. *Discernment*—Job did not need guilt; he needed friends to let him grieve.
2. *Sensitivity*—Job's friends were sensitive at first, but after seven days of silence they lost their sensitivity and chose to speak.

3. *Unconditional acceptance*—The grief sufferer needs unconditional acceptance and the freedom to speak that which is on his or her heart and mind without being judged. The moment that a grief sufferer feels the judgmental nature of another person, he or she will no longer deem it safe to share what is really on his or her heart and mind.

4. *Gentleness*—When speaking to someone who has experienced dramatic loss, or traumatic loss, one of the greatest needs that person has is to be with someone gentle and affectionate, not someone who is brash and unaffectionate.

5. *Patience*—One of the greatest skills that must be developed in grief ministry is the skill of patience. There is no timeline for recovery, and normally the greater the attachment, the greater the recovery time. Grief cannot be rushed! Every person grieves differently, and patience is often needed so that the grief sufferer can recover at his or her own pace.

Opportunities we have that allow us to do things differently ...

✦ As Job is known to be one of the oldest books of the Bible, we have advanced knowledge of Jesus Christ through the New Testament Scriptures that give us a greater advantage in ministering to the bereaved.

✦ Here is a look at what they could have done differently, if they had known then what we know now:

   o They could have *prayed* with the grief sufferer.

      ■ It does not say anything about prayer, but for grief sufferers, one of the greatest things that can be done is to pray for them and with them. Prayer invokes the presence of God in their suffering and reminds them that we have a God who hears and answers prayer (Ps. 145:16-19).

   o They could have *pointed to Jesus's* compassion for the grieving.

      ■ Remind the bereaved of Christ's compassion for those who have lost loved ones.

      ■ He never met a funeral procession that He did not stop.

      ■ He experienced great grief over the loss of a close friend.

      ■ More than likely, He experienced the death of His earthly father.

      ■ He knows how we feel, experiencing the loss of someone we have loved and lost.

   o They could have offered *reassurance* of the Lord's presence in the midst of the pain.

- If we offer spiritual words of encouragement, let us reassure the grief sufferer of the presence of the Lord in the midst of his or her pain.
  o They could have *shared Scripture.*
    - One of the most comforting things we can offer to the grieving is the reading of Scripture.
    - Psalm 23:1-6 (KJV) is still one of the most recognizable passages in the Bible.
    - John 14:1-6 (KJV) is also used frequently to comfort families during their time of grief.
  o They could have *reminded him of the victory* over death that we have through the death, burial, and resurrection of Jesus Christ.
    - Ultimately, the believer is victorious over death. What we feel when we lose a loved one is the sting of death that remains on this earth, but we must understand that death has been defeated (Heb. 2:14-15) and that we are no longer slaves to the fear of death.
    - We must avoid cold theology. Correct theology can be very cold when offered without love and compassion.
    - Correct theology will not prevent you from grieving the loss of a loved one, but correct theology will give you hope in seeing your loved one in the afterlife.
  o They could have *reminded him of heaven* and what awaits the believer.
    - Those who have been born again are in a much better place, a place where there will be no more suffering, no more death, no more pain.
    - John the Revelator says in Revelation 21:1 that there will be "no longer any sea" (NIV). For John, the sea represented separation from his loved ones on the Isle of Patmos, and he saw heaven as a place of no more separation from those he loved.

For Reflection and Discussion

A Contemporary Case Study

- I have included in the appendixes of this book a grief assessment tool. This tool is to be used to examine an individual's grief. It can be your own grief or that of someone you know. Complete the assessment and review your findings.

- I have also included a grief skills application tool. Once participants have completed the grief assessment tool, they can use this to develop a plan of care for the bereaved. As they develop a plan of care, participants will demonstrate the use of grief ministry skills in building a strategy of ministry for the grief sufferer.
- The grief assessment tool is *not* to be used for professional diagnosis but rather for the purpose of ensuring adequate care for the bereaved. Also, the purpose of the grief ministry tools is not to figure out what is "wrong" with anyone or "fix" the bereaved.
- The grief ministry tools are to help the minister or laymen see how he or she might better minister to the grief sufferer, both individually and as a church.
- Consider an actual person within your influence who may or may not be a church member, and assess that person's grief and your response to it. If that person is a church member, consider your church's overall response to his or her need.

I. Assessing grief
   - What kind of grief are we seeing in this person's life?
   - What are the normal grief symptoms he or she exhibits?
   - What stage of grief is the person experiencing?
     1. Elizabeth Kubler Ross's five stages
     2. Bowlby and Parkes' four phases of grief
     3. Rando's three phases of reaction to loss
     4. J. William Worden's four tasks of grief
   - What contemporary theories of grief affect this person's grief experience?
     1. Attachment theory
     2. Tasks of mourning
     3. Continuing bonds
     4. Dual process model
     5. Meaning reconstruction
     6. Grieving style

II. Assessing our grief ministry skills, both as individuals and as a church
   A. What did I (we) do right?
   B. What did I (we) try to do but it didn't work out very well?
   C. What did I (we) do wrong?
   D. What did I (we) lack?
   E. What opportunities do I (we) have that would allow us to do things a little differently?
   F. What do I (we) have the opportunity to do even still?

Session Five

The Practical Application of Essential Grief Ministry Skills

Developing Grief Ministry Within the Church

- It is my desire that the skills taught in this workbook are beneficial to individuals and their churches.
- I hope this workbook will inspire pastors and laity to possibly form a grief ministry team within the church that will employ the principles learned in this workshop to better minister to the bereaved, both within and outside the church.
- In order to form a grief ministry team within the church, one must affirm a few more things:
  - o Jesus is our model for ministry.
  - o Ministry must extend beyond the first week after the death.
  - o There are multiple ways to carry out ministry to the bereaved, both within and outside the church.

Practical Application of Essential Grief Ministry Skills

Our Model: Jesus Christ

The standard for ministering to the grieving has been and will always be our Lord and Savior Jesus Christ. Norman Autton states, "We learn how to minister from the one who was 'acquainted with grief.'"[203] When examining the ministry of Jesus, one has to look no further than the story of the resurrection of Lazarus in John 11:1-45 (NIV). Grief ministry in the story of Lazarus reveals several key principles that combine the theological and theoretical principles of grief ministry:

1. *Love* is the basis for ministry. Verse 5, "Now Jesus loved Martha and her sister and Lazarus."
2. Jesus had *knowledge* of his friend's death. Verse 14, "So then he told them plainly, 'Lazarus is dead.'"
3. Jesus knew ministry to the bereaved was to be a *priority*. Verse 16b, "But let us go to him."
4. Friends and family *consoled* (*comforted*) the bereaved. Verse 19, "and many Jews had come to Martha and Mary to comfort them in the loss of their brother."
5. Correct theology will *not* prevent a believer from grieving their loss. Verse 24, "Martha said to Him, 'I know that he will rise again in the resurrection on the last day.'"
6. It is normal to *blame* God for a loved one's death. Verse 32, "When Mary reached the place where Jesus was and saw him, she fell at his feet and said, 'Lord, if you had been here, my brother would not have died.'"
7. Jesus had *compassion* on Mary and Martha. Verse 33, "When Jesus saw her weeping, and the Jews who come along with her also weeping, he was deeply moved in the spirit and was troubled."
8. That *compassion* turned to *empathy*. Verse 35, "Jesus wept."
9. It was evident that Jesus *loved* them. Verse 36, "See how he loved him!"
10. It is normal to question God. Verse 37, "Could not he who opened the eyes of the blind man have kept this man from dying?"
11. Jesus did what only God could do—brought Lazarus back to life!
12. What did Jesus see in His compassion and empathy?
    + He saw every grieving mother and father, husband and wife, son and daughter, and He knew He would defeat death!

---

[203] Autton, *Pastoral Care*, 61.

✦ He saw beyond the cross to the victory that He would have over death and the grave and was determined to defeat death for eternity.

✦ 1 Corinthians 15:55-57: "O death, where is your victory? O Death, where is your sting? The sting of death is sin, and the power of sin is the law, but thanks be to God, who gives us the victory through our Lord Jesus Christ" (NKJV).

✦ Death gave Jesus His greatest ministry.

  o With Jesus as our model for ministry, death can give us our greatest ministry as well. There are many hurting people in the community around us.

  o Many people have lost loved ones, and we have the opportunity to be the love of Christ.

  o However, ministry must go beyond the first week and beyond today.

Beyond the First Week

The normal length of time that people actually minister to the grieving is very limited beyond the first week after the loss. People attend funeral visitations and memorial services within the first few days and may even fix meals to ensure the physical needs of the family are met. However, after the first week, things have a tendency to revert to normal as caregivers return to work and family, yet the world of the grief sufferer is still in complete chaos. As Jon Joyce states, "I have met more than one person who is horribly bitter toward fellow parishioners—and in some instances, a pastor because of the neglect suffered along with the grief. There was no one to help."[204] Because of the tendency to limit bereavement care to the few days surrounding the death event, it is essential that the church learn the importance of continuing ministry beyond the first week. This ministry to the grieving is essential to ensure grief sufferers have the needed support to grieve in a healthy manner as they adapt to life without their loved ones. As Harold Ivan Smith states, "Today many grievers fall through the cracks sometimes overlooked in an era of frantic busyness."[205] He adds, "Could a new widow confidently say of your congregation, 'This is my church and they're going to see that my children and I are okay?'"[206]

According to Norman Autton, "The critical time will probably last for some two or three months, and contact should be kept with the family throughout this important phase of mourning."[207] It is during this time that the grief sufferer is in the acute phase of mourning

---

[204] Joyce, *Pastor and Grief*, 19.

[205] Smith, *When You Don't Know*, 24.

[206] Smith, *When You Don't Know*, 30.

[207] Autton, *Pastoral Care*, 79.

and is in need of the most support. Individuals with adequate time for anticipatory grief may advance through the phases of grief more quickly, achieving acceptance in less time. Adversely, for individuals who had very little time for anticipatory grief, this acute phase may last much longer; therefore, the need for support will last much longer than two to three months.

To ensure the church is giving adequate support to the grief sufferer, it is important for the grief ministry team to have a plan for ministering to the bereaved beyond the first week. This plan is best achieved in three steps: (1) Assessment—The care team is to assess the bereaved to determine the level of care needed to give adequate support. (2) Development of a care plan—Once the care team has assessed the bereaved, a care plan must be developed that is unique to the individual, based on the assessment. (3) Implementation—Once the bereaved has been assessed and a care plan developed, the care team is to implement the plan to ensure that adequate care is given to the bereaved.

Beyond Today

The question that one must answer in going forward beyond today is, "How can we best carry out grief ministry to the bereaved inside and outside the church?" It is at this point that there must be a plan to carry out grief ministry. Jon L. Joyce states that "ministry to the bereaved over a period of time will amount to no ministry unless it is organized and carried through systematically." Joyce also says it is essential to "select some kind of organized plan that will help your people minister to one another in the weeks and months following the death of a loved one."[208]

In my work as a hospice chaplain and bereavement coordinator, the expectation of follow-up after the death event is thirteen months. This follow-up includes sympathy cards, telephone calls, bereavement correspondence, and personal visits. I mail a sympathy card to the primary caregiver within seven days of the death. Additionally, I schedule a bereavement assessment either by phone or by personal visit within the two to four weeks following the death. From that visit, the bereaved determines whether or not he or she desires bereavement correspondence and personal visits from me. My communication with the family or caregiver is sensitive to the concerns of the family. I speak in a sympathetic tone, offer condolences, and gently share the bereavement services offered. Though I offer follow-up bereavement measures, the nature of the follow-up is determined by the bereaved. The bereaved have the choice to accept or decline bereavement services I provide. Whether or not a person desires bereavement services

---

[208] Joyce, *The Pastor and Grief*, 129.

often depends on the level of attachment of the bereaved to me, the chaplain, prior to the death event. This will more than likely be true for a member of the church attempting grief ministry as well. If there is not a strong relationship (attachment) prior to the death event, the likelihood of a bereaved person being open to a new relationship may be diminished unless there are some commonalities.

In his book, *Comforting Those Who Grieve*, Paul Tautges outlines a sixteen-month bereavement plan.[209]

- Week 1: First personal visit with the bereaved and sympathy card
- Week 2: Phone call to the bereaved
- Week 3: Second personal visit
- Week 4: Send "praying for you" cards to the family
- Week 5: Third personal visit
- Week 6: Give the bereaved a small booklet about grief
- Week 7: Phone call
- Week 8: Send a list of comforting Scriptures
- Week 10: Fourth personal visit
- Week 12: Give the bereaved a fifth small visit
- Week 14: Phone call
- Week 16: Invite the bereaved to your home
- Months 5-11: Have some personal contact at least once a month.
- Month 12: Make personal contact, as the one-year anniversary will be a hard day
- Month 13-15: Have some personal contact at least once a month.
- Month 16: Sixth personal visit

The above care plan is an example for a grief ministry team to follow, or adjust to fit their ministry context. The focus of such a plan is the ministry to the bereaved, understanding that a complex plan for follow-up is more likely to be acted upon than no plan at all. The best of intentions seldom come to pass if there is no plan and no commitment to follow a plan.

---

[209] Paul Tautges, *Comforting Those Who Grieve* (Carlisle, PA: Day One Publications, 2009), 104-106.

For Reflection and Discussion

Commitment to Ministry
- My original goal in writing this workbook was to train members of my congregation in grief ministry skills so that my church could better minister to the grieving. It is my desire to educate and equip individuals in the faith community with grief ministry skills that they might use to better minister to the bereaved.
- I am hopeful that individuals will commit to participating in grief ministry teams within their local church, which goes beyond attending funerals and carrying food to the families in the first week.
- I also desire to see individuals ministering beyond the walls of the church. As Harold Ivan Smith states, "Grief sharing is kingdom work."[210]

---

[210] Smith, *When You Don't Know What to Say*, 111.

Attachment A

Grief Assessment Tool

Name: _____ Date: _____

Deceased: _____ Relationship to loss: _____

Briefly describe the loss: _____

_____

1. Types of grief evident in the bereaved (circle all that apply)

   A. Normal and unresolved grief

Abbreviated	Absent	Acute	Anticipatory
Chronic	Compound	Conflicted	Converted
Delayed	Disenfranchised	Distorted	Inhibited
Normal	Unanticipated	Unresolved	

2. Symptoms of grief evident in the bereaved (circle all that apply)

A. Emotional symptoms

Sadness	Anger	Guilt	Anxiety
Loneliness	Fatigue	Helplessness	Shock
Yearning	Emancipation	Numbness	

B. Physical symptoms

Hollowness in stomach	Tightness in chest	Tightness in throat
Oversensitivity to noise	Breathlessness	Weakness in muscles
Lack of energy	Dry mouth	

C. Cognitive symptoms

Disbelief	Confusion	Preoccupation	Sense of presence
Hallucinations			

D. Behavioral symptoms:

Absentminded behavior	Appetite disturbances	Avoids reminders
Crying	Dreams of the deceased	Restless hyperactivity
Searching and calling out	Sighing	Sleep disturbances
Social withdrawal	Treasuring objects	Visiting places as reminders

3. Contemporary theory of grief

A. Attachment theory

Level of attachment (circle the level that best represents the attachment.)

Low … … … … … … … … … … Medium … … … … … … … … … … High

B. Meaning reconstruction

Level of meaning reconstruction (Circle the level that best represents the reconstruction of meaning)

Life's narrative changes:

Low … … … … … … … … … … … Medium … … … … … … … … … … … High

4. Stages, phases, and tasks of grief (check all that apply)

A. Elizabeth Kubler-Ross's Five Stages
    1. Denial and isolation (shock)   ____
    2. Anger   ____
    3. Bargaining   ____
    4. Depression   ____
    5. Acceptance   ____

B. John Bowlby's Four Phases
    1. Numbness   ____
    2. Yearning and searching   ____
    3. Disorganization and despair   ____
    4. Reorganization   ____

C. Theresa Rando's Phases
    1. Avoidance phase   ____
    2. Confrontation phase   ____
    3. Reestablishment phase   ____

D. William Worden's Four Tasks
    1. To accept the loss   ____
    2. To experience the pain of grief   ____
    3. To adjust to an environment without the deceased   ____
    4. To withdraw emotional energy and reinvest it   ____

    E. Bereavement Trajectories
        1. Resilient   ____
        2. Struggling but recovers   ____
        3. Complicated/unresolved   ____

5. Summary of assessment

Summary of facts from the above listings:

    1. _____
    2. _____
    3. _____
    4. _____
    5. _____

6. Assessing level of care that the bereaved needs to ensure that the bereaved is properly ministered to:

Low … … … … … … … … … … … Medium … … … … … … … … … … … High

Why have you chosen this level?

Attachment B

Grief Skills Application Tool

Name: _____ Date: _____

Type of loss:_____

Level of attachment:_____

Length of time since loss occurred: _____

What stage, phase, or task is the bereaved in: _____

Understanding that the stronger the attachment the greater the need for ministry to the bereaved, how can one apply the grief ministry skills learned in this course to better minister to the bereaved? (This question needs to be answered both individually and as a church.)

What ministry skills would best attend to the grief sufferer's needs at this time?

Primary grief ministry skills (circle the ones you feel are most needed)

Companioning	Empathy	Gifting	Listening
Prayer	Presence	Scripture Sensitive	

Secondary skills (circle the ones you feel are most needed)

Acceptance	Acts of kindness	Awareness	Care
Comfort	Compassion	Helping	Love/mercy
Reassurance	Silence	Sympathy	Talking

The Practice of Primary Grief Ministry Skills

A. How can I practice the skill of *companioning* in his or her grief?

_____

_____

a. Remember the 11 Tenets of Companioning:[211]
   i. Companioning is about being present in another person's pain.
   ii. Companioning is about going to the wilderness of the soul with another human being.
   iii. Companioning is about honoring the spirit; it is not about focusing on the intellect.
   iv. Companioning is about listening with the heart, not analyzing with the head.
   v. Companioning is about bearing witness to the struggles of others; it is not about judging or directing these struggles.
   vi. Companioning is about walking alongside; it is not about leading.
   vii. Companioning means discovering the gifts of sacred silence, not filling up every moment with words.
   viii. Companioning is about being still; it is not about frantic movement forward.

---

[211] Alan D. Wolfelt, *The Handbook for Companioning the Mourner* (Fort Collins, CO: Companion Press, 2009), 13-104.

     ix.   Companioning is about respecting disorder and confusion; it is not about imposing order and logic.

     x.   Companioning is about learning from others; it is not about teaching them.

     xi.   Companioning is about curiosity; it is not about expertise.

B. How can I practice the skill of *empathy* in his or her grief?

     a.   Four major benefits of empathy that bears witness without bringing judgment:[212]

        i.   Empathetic communication is a foundation upon which you establish a companion relationship with the mourner.

        ii.   The mourner who feels empathetically understood and not judged is more likely to risk sharing deep, soul-based encounters with grief.

        iii.   The mourner's experience of your genuine effort and commitment to understand creates a trusting, low-threatening environment that negates the need for self-protection and isolation.

        iv.   The communication of empathy encourages self-exploration in the mourner, a prerequisite for compassionate self-understanding and, eventually, movement toward reconciliation.

C. How can I practice the skill of *gifting* in his or her grief?

     a.   One of the easiest ways to express love and encouragement to the grief suffer is that of a simple gift.

     b.   Frequently purchased gifts for the bereaved in honor or memory of their lost loved ones:

        i.   flowers

        ii.   cards

        iii.   pottery

        iv.   a book about grief

---

[212] Wolfelt, *Handbook for Companioning*, 62.

D. How can I practice the skill of *listening* in his or her grief?

_____

_____

    a. When it comes to ministering to the grieving, "sympathetic listening will always help to release grief."[213]

    b. "There are three things you can do to help someone. The first is to listen, the second is to listen. The third is to listen more."[214]

    c. "Every griever has three essential needs: to find words to express the loss, to say the words aloud, and to know the words have been heard."[215]

    d. When the caregiver "listens permissively, he opens the way for the grief sufferer to tell his story and develop his own insights as quickly as possible."[216]

E. How can I practice the skill of *prayer* in his or her grief?

_____

_____

    a. Remember, "A helper prays for the grieving, and a helper prays with the grieving."[217]

    b. How to pray for those who lost loved ones:

        i. Pray that the family can feel the presence of the Lord, knowing He will never leave us nor forsake us.

        ii. Pray that the Lord will comfort their hearts and minds in Christ Jesus as only He can.

        iii. Pray that the Lord will provide them strength to endure the loss.

        iv. Pray, thanking God for their friendship, their family, and their faith in Jesus Christ as Lord and Savior.

F. How can I practice the skill of *presence* in his or her grief?

_____

_____

---

[213] Norman Autton, *The Pastoral Care of the Bereaved* (London: William Clowes and Sons, Limited London and Beccles, 1967), 60.

[214] Harold Ivan Smith, *When You Don't Know What to Say* (Kansas City, KS; Beacon Hill Press, 2012), 17.

[215] Smith, *When You Don't Know*, 57.

[216] Smith, *When You Don't Know*, 37.

[217] Smith, *When You Don't Know*, 81.

a. Presence is simply being present in the life of the grief sufferer, as "no one should walk alone through the valley of the shadow of death."[218]

b. Presence is as simple as "Show up, sit down, and stay a while."[219]

c. It is comforting to the grief suffer to know "there is someone who walks with him, who knows the hurt and the painful reminders of days that used to be, who is standing by."[220]

d. "Blessed are those who mourn, for they will be comforted by God through people like you."[221]

G. How can I practice the skill of using *Scripture* in his or her grief?

_____

_____

a. One of the greatest comforts to Christians is a timely read Scripture passage in the midst of their sorrow.

b. Ministers "best accomplish spiritual care through prayer and the ministry of the Word that is intentionally focused on God's desirer and care."[222]

c. The most frequently used passages are: Psalm 23, Psalm 46, Psalm 121, Matthew 5:4, John 14:1-3, Hebrews 13:5, and Revelation 21:4-6.

H. How can I practice the skill of being *sensitive* in his or her grief?

_____

_____

a. Paul Tautges suggests a five-step process in which being sensitive is a necessity. His process includes the following actions:

  i. Establish understanding with a tender touch and a few nonintrusive questions to determine immediate needs, discerning any immediate needs or fears.

  ii. Show compassion by empathizing with the person's pain, being sensitive to immediate needs, and always speaking graciously.

  iii. Obtain permission to help where help is needed by gently asking for permission without being bombastic.

---

[218] Smith, *When You Don't Know*, 14.

[219] Smith, *When You Don't Know*, 16.

[220] C. Charles Bachmann, *Ministering to the Grief Sufferer* (Englewood Cliffs, NJ: Prentice-Hall, Inc. 1964), 32.

[221] Bachmann, *Ministering to the Grief Sufferer*, 112.

[222] Brian Croft, *Caring for Widows* (Wheaton, IL: Crossway Books, 2015), 88.

    iv.   Dispense biblical comfort and hope with appropriate Scriptures and offer to pray with the person.

    v.   Give the person assurance of your continued prayers and support.[223]

The Practice of Secondary Grief Ministry Skills

I.   How can I practice the skill of *acceptance* in his or her grief?

_____

_____

    a.   To accept the grief suffer where he or she is, offer the grief sufferer a safe place to share his or her experience. If a person does not feel his or her grief is welcome, then that person will not feel welcome. Acceptance is important to the grief sufferer's healing and resolution.

J.   How can I practice the skill of *acts of kindness* in his or her grief?

_____

_____

    a.   Often immediately after a loss, the grief sufferer is in shock and limited in his or her ability to do some of the simplest of things.

    b.   If the grief sufferer is open to you being in the home, often simple household chores can be of assistance. Sweeping the floors, helping with laundry, washing dishes, or even running errands can be extremely helpful.

K.   How can I practice the skill of *awareness* in his or her grief?

_____

_____

    a.   The need for awareness does not mean that the helper has the right to be intrusive and encroach on the personal life of the grief suffer.

    b.   It merely means that the helper needs to be aware of pertinent information that would help him or her minister to the physical, social, emotional, and spiritual needs of the grief sufferer.

---

[223] Paul Tautges, *Comfort Those Who Grieve: Ministering God's Grace in Times of Loss* (Carlisle, PA: Day One Publications, 2009), 110-111.

    c.   The helper must be informed in order to help meet the needs of the grief sufferer. A grief helper cannot attend to the needs of the grief sufferer if he or she is not aware of the need.

L. How can I practice the skill of *caring* in his or her grief?

    _____

    _____

    a.   The basis of all grief ministry is an attitude of caring.
    b.   Sharing in someone's grief "looks for an opportunity to actively care."[224]
    c.   Though much has changed in contemporary society, the death event is still an excellent opportunity to show others that we care.

M. How can I practice the skill of *comfort* in his or her grief?

    _____

    _____

    a.   Remember Nancy Guthrie's "Ten Things to Do to Comfort the Bereaved":
        o   Don't try to "fix" their grief but do say something.
        o   Don't tell a story about your own or someone else's loss.
        o   Be a welcome companion in grief, regardless of how well you know them.
        o   Give them permission to cry.
        o   Proactively meet practical needs.
        o   Use their loved one's name in conversation.
        o   If you knew the person who died, tell that person's grieving loved one a story about him or her.
        o   If possible, simply show up at the visitation, the funeral, and beyond.
        o   Invite them to talk about their grief and their loved one who died.
        o   Reach out to grieving members of your congregation on the anniversaries of their loved ones' deaths.

N. How can I practice the skill of *compassion* in his or her grief?

    _____

    _____

---

[224] Smith, *When You Don't Know What to Say*, 17.

    a.   To show compassion to those who mourn the loss of a loved one is the very essence of Christ in the believer.

    b.   As Jesus was full of compassion, so should we. Brian Croft states, "such compassion (as Jesus) and love ought to be freely, cheerfully, and willingly displayed."[225]

O. How can I practice the skill of *helping* in his or her grief?

_____

_____

    a.   "Blessed are those who show up and anticipate what needs to be done."[226]

    b.   Grief sharers ask three questions: What can I do? What can I not do? What shall I do first?[227]

P. How can I practice the skill of *love* in his or her grief?

_____

_____

    a.   Caring for grief sufferers demands sacrificial love, a love that puts others first, above a person's own needs.

    b.   There must be a "genuine love for another, that is a non-possessive love that accepts others just as they are and desires the best for them."[228]

    c.   It is important that the love of Christ flow through the caregiver to the grief sufferer, to "make the love of God real to the person you visit."[229]

Q. How can I practice the skill of *reassurance* in his or her grief?

_____

_____

    a.   Paul Tautges suggests five reassurances that one can give grief sufferers.[230]
        o   Reassure them that grieving is not a sin.
        o   Reassure them of the character of God.

---

[225] Croft, *Caring for Widows*, 26.

[226] Smith, *When You Don't Know*, 66.

[227] Smith, *When You Don't Know*, 67.

[228] Smith, *When You Don't Know What to Say*, 89-90.

[229] Smith, *When You Don't Know What to Say*, 75.

[230] Tautges, *Comfort Those Who Grieve*, 114-115.

      ○   Reassure them through the ministry of your presence and prayers.

      ○   Reassure them of the need to let others serve them.

      ○   Reassure them that God will walk through the future with them.

R. How can I practice the skill of *silence* in his or her grief?

_____

_____

    a. "Sometimes ministering to others simply means being quiet."[231]

    b. The truth is that sometimes, "sitting alone in shared silence can be healing for both the griever and the helper."[232]

S. How can I practice the skill of *sympathy* in his or her grief?

_____

_____

    a. To sympathize means to "feel along with."[233]

    b. One of the easiest ways to display sympathy is that of attending the funeral visitation or the funeral ceremony.

T. How can I practice the skill of *talking*?

_____

_____

    a. "There are no experts on grief when it comes to composing words."[234]

    b. Two easily asked nonintrusive statements to initiate conversation:
        i.   "Would you like to talk about it?"
        ii. "Tell me how things are."

    c. Avoid clichés:
        i.   the generic— "Time heals all wounds."
        ii. the spiritual—"God never puts more on us than we can handle."
        iii. the admonitions—"Be strong for your children."

---

[231] Smith, *When You Don't Know What to Say*, 48.
[232] Smith, *When You Don't Know What to Say*, 49.
[233] Bachmann, *Ministering to the Grief Sufferer*, 32
[234] Smith, *When You Don't Know What to Say*, 46.

         iv.   the laudatory—"You're holding up so well."[235]

   d. Wrong things to say to a bereaved person

      a.   "I know how you feel."

      b.   "You shouldn't feel that way."

      c.   "It was God's will."

      d.   "You've got to get on with your life."

      e.   "You've got to be strong."

      f.   "God took him or her."

      g.   "God needed him or her."

      h.   "You should be over that by now."

      i.   "You can have other children." (When someone has lost a child.)

      j.   "God is testing you."

      k.   "Good will come out of it."

      l.   "It's for the best."

      m. "Just turn it over to God." (Implies if you have faith, you should not grieve.)

      n.   "You're so lucky your loved one is in heaven."

      o.   "God never gives you more than you can handle."

      p.   "You are not handling it right."

      q.   "Time heals all wounds."

      r.   "You'll get over it."

      s.   "You shouldn't talk/think about it."

      t.   "He's in hell." (In the context of suicide.)

      u.   "How are you doing?" (Unless you really want to know.)

      v.   Anything that implies guilt!

      w. "I could never handle it like you are. I'd go insane."

---

[235] Smith, *When You Don't Know What to Say*, 47.

Attachment C

Theological Dimensions of Death and Grief Ministry

Doctrines Related to Death, Grief, and Grief Ministry

The Doctrine of the Bible

- The Holy Bible is the final authority for the study of God and is the foundation of all Christian doctrines.
- Understanding the validity of Scripture for God's self-revelation, I see the Bible as the sole authority for faith and practice, as revealed in the Scriptures of the Old Testament and the New Testament. Thus, the Bible is the foundation for all Christian beliefs and ministries.
- The 1963 *Baptist Faith and Message* expresses this biblical authority clearly: "The Holy Bible was written by men divinely inspired and is the record of God's revelation of himself to man. It is a perfect treasure of divine instruction. It has God for its author, salvation for its end, and truth, without any mixture of error, for its matter. It reveals the principles by which God judges us; and therefore is, and will remain to the end of the world, the true center of Christian union, and the supreme standard by which all human conduct, creeds, and religious opinions should be tried."[236]

---

[236] Russell H. Dilday Jr., *The Doctrine of Biblical Authority* (Nashville: Convention Press, 1982), 3031.

- The Bible is to be viewed as the sole authority for all faith and practice because it is inspired by God. Apostle Paul said in 2 Timothy 3:16, "All Scripture is God-breathed and is useful for teaching, rebuking, correcting and training in righteousness"(NIV).
- Wayne Grudem writes, "It is helpful for us to learn that the Bible is historically accurate, that it is internally consistent, that it contains prophecies that have been fulfilled hundreds of years later, that it has influenced the course of human history more than any other book, that it has continued changing the lives of millions of individuals throughout its history, that through it people come to find salvation, that it has a majestic beauty and a profound depth of teaching unmatched by any other book, and that it claims hundreds of times over to be God's very words."[237]
- Thus, the Bible continues to be the living Word of God, as the author of Hebrews 4:12 states, "For the word of God is living and active, and sharper than any two edged sword, even penetrating as far as the division of soul and spirit, of both joints and marrow; and able to judge the thoughts and intentions of the heart" (NASB).
- As the authoritative Word of God, the Bible is the sole authority for truth, hope, and encouragement.
  - This is especially important when faced with the reality of death and loss, as no one is immune to losing loved ones and experiencing grief.
  - Hope and encouragement are best achieved as theological doctrines that are believed and practiced in such a way that man is prepared to face death with faith through the saving work of Jesus Christ, the comfort of the Holy Spirit, and the love of the church.
  - As such, the Bible teaches the essential theological doctrines that are pertinent to man's understanding of God, humanity, sin, salvation, Christ, the Holy Spirit, and the church.

The Doctrine of God

- The doctrine of the study of God is called theology.
- When experiencing the loss of a loved one, even people with strong faiths may question God as they grieve their loss. Questions commonly asked may include, "Where was God?" and "Why did God allow my loss?" and "If God answers prayer, why didn't he answer my prayers for my loved one?"

---

[237] Wayne Grudem, *Systematic Theology: An Introduction to Biblical Doctrine* (Grand Rapids, MI: Zondervan, 1994), 78.

- During times of grief, it is important for those suffering the loss of a loved one to have a strong theological foundation. It is also important for those ministering to grief sufferers to have a strong biblical concept of God.
- Confusion often abounds in cultures where many ideas and opinions exist about God. Because much confusion exists in the present culture, it is important to understand the biblical concept of God. Understanding the biblical concept of God leads us to a proper understanding of the doctrine of God, which is central to having a proper understanding of God.
- To better understand God, various writers and authors have tried to define the attributes of God. These attributes are best distinguished as either incommunicable or communicable.[238]
  - The *incommunicable* attributes are "those attributes that God does not share or 'communicate' to others." Examples of the incommunicable attributes include God's eternality, God's unchangeableness, and God's omnipresence.
  - The *communicable* attributes of God are those God shares or "communicates with us." Examples of the communicable attributes of God include Him being loving, merciful, and just.
- How both types of attributes relate to grief ministry may be best understood with the example of God being both infinite and personal.[239]
  - Unlike man, who is finite and has many limitations, God is "infinite in that he is not subject to any of the limitations of humanity."
  - At the same time, God is also personal: "He interacts with us as a person, and we can relate to him as persons."
  - Because God relates to man as personal, man can "pray to him, worship him, obey him, and love him, and he can speak to us, rejoice with us, and love us."
  - Additionally, these incommunicable and communicable attributes can be further understood by examining God's omnipresence (incommunicable) and God's omniscience (communicable).
- Omniscient—Because God is omniscient, he has perfect knowledge of all things, as John says in 1 John 3:20, God "knows all things" (CSB). Thus, God knows everything about man and his struggles with the loss of loved ones.
- Omnipresent—Also, because God is omnipresent, He is not confined to time and space. This incommunicable attribute means that God's presence is everywhere.

---

[238] Grudem, *Systematic Theology*, 156.
[239] Grudem, *Systematic Theology*, 167.

Wayne Grudem states it best as he says, "There is nowhere in the entire universe, on land or sea, in heaven or in hell, where one can flee from God's presence."[240]

- Because God is both omniscient and omnipresent, He knows everything the grief sufferer is experiencing, and His presence is available to the grief sufferer in his or her time of need.

- Omnipotent—Additionally, we must understand God's omnipotence. This communicable attribute is derived from two Latin words: *omni*, meaning "all," and *potens*, meaning "powerful"; thus, the two words together mean "all-powerful." Understanding that God is all-powerful, ever-present, and all-knowing and that He is a good, loving, and merciful God is essential to individuals suffering the loss of a loved one and those ministering to grief sufferers.

The Doctrine of Christ

- The doctrine of the study of Christ is called "Christology."
- To further understand the reality of God, understanding the person and work of Jesus Christ is essential. A summarization of the biblical teachings about the person of Christ can be succinctly stated as "Jesus Christ was fully God and fully man in one person."[241]
- Being fully human, He sympathized and suffered along with those He loved and lost. Being fully divine, He had a greater purpose: to redeem sinful humanity. In Galatians 4:4-5, Paul says of the work of Christ, "But when the fullness of time had come, God sent forth his Son, born of woman, born under the law, to redeem those under the law, so that we might receive adoption as sons" (NKJV).
- The redemption of sinful humanity could only be accomplished through the work of Christ, in His life and death as an atoning sacrifice for man's sinfulness. Wayne Grudem says of Christ's atonement, "The atonement is the work Christ did in his life and death to earn our salvation."[242]
- Christ lived a life of perfect obedience to God, and He fulfilled all the requirements of the law. His obedience was such that He never did anything wrong, and He did everything right. Scripture repeatedly claims that Christ's death was a sacrificial payment for the sins of humanity. God's greater purpose for Jesus was the work of redemption of sinful humanity. In the redeeming work of Christ, Jesus died as a

---

[240] Grudem, *Systematic Theology*, 174.
[241] Grudem, *Systematic Theology*, 529.
[242] Grudem, *Systematic Theology*, 568.

sacrifice and a propitiation for the sins of men. The sacrificial death of Jesus Christ appeased the wrath of God toward man's sinfulness, and Jesus was resurrected to prove His sacrifice was accepted by God.

- Through the redeeming work of Christ's life, death, and resurrection, God has provided salvation to sinful humanity. This salvation is free to all who will believe and receive Christ by faith. In John 3:16, John states, "For God so loved the world that He gave His only begotten Son, that whosoever believes in Him should not perish but have everlasting life" (NKJV).
- The doctrine of Christology provides hope for those who have placed their faith in Jesus Christ for salvation. Because of Christ's life, death, resurrection, and exaltation, we have an eternal hope to combat the struggles of this life. Jesus Himself said, "I am the resurrection and the life. Whoever believes in me, though he die, yet shall he live" John 11:35 (ESV).
- According to Paul Tautges, "The central message of the Bible is one of hope—that the death of one can bring life to ministry. ... He (God) brings spiritual life out of the death of His only begotten Son, Jesus Christ."[243]

The Doctrine of the Holy Spirit

- The doctrine of the Holy Spirit is referred to in Christian systematic theology as the doctrine of pneumatology. It is derived from two Greek words: *pneuma*, meaning "breath" or "wind," and *logos*, meaning "word."
- The doctrine of the Holy Spirit refers to the existence of God as a Spirit.
- In the study of God, the Holy Spirit is fully and equally God. As such, the Holy Spirit shares all the attributes of God. Thus, the incommunicable and communicable attributes of God exist in the person of the Holy Spirit. Wayne Grudem says of the Holy Spirit that "God eternally exists as three persons, Father, Son, and Holy Spirit, and each person is fully God, and there is one God."[244]
- Thus, the role of the Holy Spirit in the world is to "manifest the active presence of God in the world."[245]
- This is of primary importance when experiencing or ministering to those who have experienced the loss of a loved one. Since the Holy Spirit is fully God and can manifest

---

[243] Paul Tautges, *Comfort Those Who Grieve: Ministering God's Grace in Times of Loss* (Carlisle, PA: Day One Publications, 2009), 69.

[244] Grudem, *Systematic Theology* 226.

[245] Grudem, *Systematic Theology*, 634.

His presence, "He resides within believers, bringing fellowship with God the Father and the Son."[246]

- One specific role of the Holy Spirit essential for grief ministry is that of the Holy Spirit being the "Comforter." In John 14:16, Jesus says, "And I will pray the Father, and he shall give you another Comforter, and that he may abide with you forever" (KJV). In this passage of Scripture, Jesus refers to the Holy Spirit as "Comforter." Other versions of the Bible translate the word as "Counselor" (CSB), "Helper" (NASB), and "Advocate" (NIV).

- The root meaning is derived from the Greek rendering *paraclete,* which means "to come along side of."[247] Jesus was promising His disciples that the Holy Spirit would come alongside them and be a comforter, counselor, helper, and advocate. Additionally, this "Comforter" is promised to abide "with us forever." This literally means that the Holy Spirit is available and present to every believer, manifesting God's presence. The Holy Spirit comes alongside grief sufferers in the middle of their time of grieving.

- The doctrine of pneumatology, while important to grief sufferers, is also of great importance to those ministering to them. The very presence of God is manifest in the Holy Spirit and is available to those suffering the loss of loved ones. He is also available to help the individuals attempting to minister to the grief sufferers. He can guide and direct the words and actions of those ministering in the name of Jesus to establish the loving presence of Christ through the companionship of a brother or sister in Christ.

The Doctrine of Humanity and Sin

- In studying grief ministry, establishing the relationship between humanity and sin is essential. When one considers that death is a consequence of humankind's sin and grief is a consequence of death, then there is a direct relationship between humanity, sin, death, and grief.

- The doctrine of humanity is the belief that man was created by God, and as such, man is God's special creation. Scripture attests that humankind was made in the image of God. Genesis 1:27 states, "So God created man in his own image, in the image of God he created him; male and female he created them" (KJV).

---

[246] Malcom B. Yarnell, III, "The Person and Work of the Holy Spirit," in *A Theology for the Church,* ed. Daniel Akin (Nashville: Broadman and Holman Academic, 2007), 619.

[247] Yarnell, "Person and Work," 619.

- God created humanity in His image and gave them the responsibility to live in relationship with Him and "to reflect the image of God to God, others, and creation."[248] God created man for a special relationship with God, and man enjoyed perfect fellowship with God prior to the fall.

- The doctrine of humanity intersects with the doctrine of sin at the point that Adam and Eve sinned in the Garden of Eden. Genesis 2:16-17 states, "And the Lord God commanded the man, "You are free to eat from any tree in the garden; but you must not eat from the tree of the knowledge of good and evil, for when you eat of it you will surely die" (NIV). Though God created Adam and Even in the His image and they enjoyed perfect fellowship, they violated God's command to not eat from the tree of knowledge, thus committing the first sin. Wayne Grudem defines sin as "any failure to conform to the moral law of God in act, attitude, or nature."[249] Adam and Eve's willful violation of God's direct command was sin, and this sin broke their perfect relationship with God.

- The Bible teaches that since Adam and Eve's original sin in the Garden of Eden, their sinful nature has been passed down to every person born. Paul stated in Romans 3:23, "For all have sinned and fall short of the glory of God" (NIV).

- The writers of the Holy Bible use multiple words to describe sin: depravity, error, guilt, godlessness, ignorance, iniquity, lawless, etc. However, the most common meaning for sin is "missing the mark." This meaning for sin can be found in both the Old Testament and the New Testament. In the Old Testament, there are approximately six hundred occurrences of the Hebrew word *chata'*, which means "missing the mark." In the New Testament, there are approximately three hundred occurrences of the word *hamartano*, which means "missing the mark."[250] Thus, one can surmise that a person is guilty of sin when they miss the mark by not meeting God's expectations for human attitudes and actions.

- It is easy to see the association between the doctrine of humanity and the doctrine of sin, as man was created to reflect the image of God in His greatest creation, yet that image is flawed by man's sinfulness. Once one understands how the two doctrines correlate, several consequences are obviously associated with them.

- The most obvious consequence of sin was revealed to Adam and Eve in relation to the command to not eat of the tree of knowledge of good and evil, as the Lord

---

[248] R. Stanton Norman, "Human Sinfulness," in *A Theology for the Church*, ed. Daniel Akin (Nashville: Broadman and Holman Academic, 2007), 411.

[249] Grudem, *Systematic* Theology, 490.

[250] Norman, *Human Sinfulness*, 417.

warned them, "For when you shall eat of it you will surely die" (Gen. 2:17 NIV). Furthermore, Paul clearly states in Romans 6:23, "For the wages of sin is death" (NIV). Understanding that death is a natural consequence of man's sinfulness, it can further be understood that grief is a natural consequence of death. Thus, a direct relationship exists between humanity, sin, death, and grief.

- Though sin disrupted man's special relationship with God and led to death and grief, reconciliation with God was made possible through the person and work of Christ. Through the atoning sacrifice of Jesus Christ, God offers forgiveness of sin and a restored relationship with Him.

- This restored relationship, received by grace through repentance and faith in Christ, offers many benefits. One of the greatest benefits that is essential in the experience of the grief sufferer or the person ministering to grief sufferers is the promise of eternal life. Jesus expressed this reality to His good friend Mary upon the death of her brother. As He said in John 11:35, "I am the resurrection and the life. He who believes in me will live, even though he dies; and whoever lives and believes in me will never die" (NIV). The assurance of eternal life is one of the greatest sources of comfort when experiencing the loss of a loved one. As Paul Tautges states, "Death is not the end. For some it is the beginning of eternity in the presence of God because their trust was in the person and work of Jesus Christ alone. This is how God brings life out of death."[251]

---

[251] Tautges, *Comfort Those Who Grieve*, 72.

Selected Bibliography

Books

Akin, Daniel L., ed. *A Theology for the Church*. Nashville: Broadman and Holman Academic, 2007.

Autton, Norman. *The Pastoral Care of the Bereaved*. London: William Clowes and Sons, 1967.

Bachmann, C. Charles. *Ministering to the Grief Suffer*. Englewood Cliffs, NJ: Prentice-Hall, Inc., 1964.

Bailey-Rug, Cynthia. *Emerging from the Chrysalis*. Morrisville, NC: Lulu Publishing, 2012.

Croft, Brian and Austin Walker. *Caring for Widows*. Wheaton, IL: Crossway, 2015.

Dilday, Russell H. Jr., *The Doctrine of Biblical Authority*. Nashville: Convention Press, 1982.

Doka, Kenneth J., ed. *Grief Is a Journey: Finding Your Path Through Loss*. New York: Atria Books, 2016.

———. *Life Beyond Loss*. Acworth, GA: Guideline Publications, 2014.

———. *Living with Grief After Sudden Loss: Suicide, Homicide, Accident, Heart Attack, Stroke*. Washington, DC: Taylor & Francis Publishers, 1996.

Doka, Kenneth J. and Terry L. Martin. *Grieving Beyond Gender*. New York: Taylor & Francis Group, 2010.

Guthrie, David, and Nancy Guthrie. *When Your Family's Lost a Loved One*. Carol Springs, IL: Tyndale House Publishers, Inc., 2008.

Grudem, Wayne. *Systematic Theology: An Introduction to Biblical Doctrine*. Grand Rapids, MI: Zondervan, 1994.

Hunt, June. *Grief: Living at Peace with Loss*. Torrance, CA: Rose Publishing, 2013.

James, John W., and Russell Friedman. *The Grief Recovery Handbook*. New York: Harper Collins Publishers, 2009.

Joyce, Jon L. *The Pastor and Grief*. Lima, OH: C.S.S. Publishing Co. Inc., 1973.

Kelley, Charles S. Jr., Richard Land, and R. Albert Mohler Jr., *The Baptist Faith and Message*. Nashville: LifeWay Press, 2007.

Kelley, Melissa M. *Grief: Contemporary Theory and the Practice of Ministry*. Minneapolis: Fortress Press, 2010.

Kubler-Ross, Elisabeth. *Questions and Answers on Death and Dying*. New York: Macmillan Publishing Co., 1974.

Lewis, C.S. *A Grief Observed*. New York: Harper Collins Publishers, 1996.

Meagher, David K., and David E. Balk, eds. *Handbook of Thanatology*. New York: Routledge, 2013.

Neimeyer, Robert A., ed. *Techniques in Grief Therapy*. New York: Routledge, 2016.

Neimeyer, Robert A., Darcy L. Harris, Howard R. Winokuer, and Gordon F. Thorton, eds. *Grief and Bereavement in Contemporary Society: Bridging Research and Practice*. New York: Routledge, Taylor and Francis Group, 2011.

Neimeyer, Robert A. and Diana C. Sands; eds. Robert A. Neimeyer, Darcy L. Harris, Howard R. Winokuer, and Gordon F. Thorton, *"Meaning Reconstruction in Bereavement" in Grief and Bereavement in Contemporary Society*. (New York, NY: Routledge Taylor & Francis Group, 2011), 11.

Rando, Therese A. *Grief, Dying and Death: Clinical Interventions for Caregivers*. Champaign, IL: Research Press, 1984.

Smith, Harold Ivan. *A Decembered Grief*. Kansas City, KS: Beacon Hill Press, 2011.

———. *When You Don't Know What to Say: How to Help Your Grieving Friends*. Kansas City, KS: Beacon Hill Press, 2012.

Sunderland, Ronald. *Getting Through Grief: Caregiving by Congregations*. Nashville: Abingdon Press, 1993.

Tautges, Paul. *Comfort Those Who Grieve: Ministering God's Grace in Times of Loss*. Carlisle, PA: Day One Publications, 2009.

Toole, Mary. *Handbook for Chaplains*. New York, NJ: Paulist Press, 2006.

Westberg, Granger E., *Good Grief*. Minneapolis: Fortress Press, 2011.

Wiersbe, Warren, and David Wiersbe. *Ministering to the Mourning: A Practical Guide for Pastors, Church Leaders, and Other Caregivers.* Chicago: Moody Publishers, 2006.

Williams, Donna Reilly, and JoAnn Sturzl. *Grief Ministry: Helping Others Mourn.* San Jose, CA: Resource Publications, 1992.

Wolfelt, Alan D. *Death and Grief a Guide for Clergy.* Muncie, IN: Accelerated Development Inc. Publishers, 1988.

———. *The Handbook for Companioning the Mourner: Eleven Essential Principles.* Fort Collins, CO: Companion Press, 2009.

Worden, J. William. *Grief Counseling and Grief Therapy,* 5th ed. New York: Springer Publishing Company, 2018.

———. *Grief Counseling and Grief Therapy,* 4th ed. New York: Springer Publishing Company, 2009.

Wright, H. Norman. *Experiencing Grief.* Nashville: B&H Group, 2004.

———. *Experiencing the Loss of a Family Member.* Grand Rapids, MI: Bethany House Publishers, 2014.

———. *Recovering from Losses in Life.* Grand Rapids, MI: Revell, 2006.

———. *Reflections of a Grieving Spouse.* Eugene, OR: Harvest House Publishers, 2009.

Periodicals

Kessler, David. "Moving Through Grief: How Kubler-Ross's Model Can Help Clients Heal." *Psychotherapy Networker* 6, July/August 2016.

Peterson, Tom O., and David D. Van Fleet. "The Ongoing Legacy of R.L. Katz: An Updated Typology of Management Skills." *Management Decision* 42, no. 10 (2004).

Strobe, Margaret and Henk Schut. "The Dual Process Model of Coping with Bereavement: A Decade On." *OMEGA—Journal of Death and Dying* 61, no. 4 (2010).

Printed in the United States
by Baker & Taylor Publisher Services